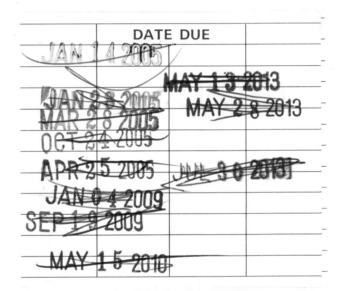

SCIENCE ACTIVITIES

ELECTRICITY

— AND —

MAGNETISM

VOLUME 1

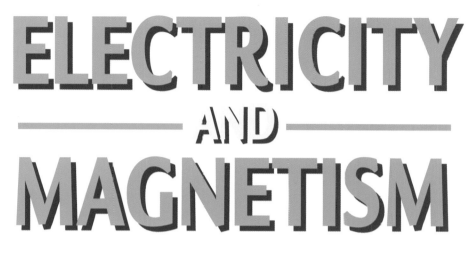

Chris Woodford

GROLIER
EDUCATIONAL

Published 2002 by Grolier Educational
Sherman Turnpike,
Danbury, Connecticut 06816

© 2002 Brown Partworks Limited

FOR BROWN PARTWORKS

Project editor:	Lisa Magloff
Deputy editor:	Jane Scarsbrook
Text editors:	Caroline Beattie
Designers:	Joan Curtis, Alison Gardner
Picture researcher:	Liz Clachan
Illustrations:	Darren Awuah, Mark Walker
Index:	Kay Ollerenshaw
Design manager:	Lynne Ross
Production manager:	Matt Weyland
Managing editor:	Bridget Giles
Editorial director:	Anne O'Daly
Consultant:	Martyn D. Wheeler, PhD
	University of Leicester

Printed and bound in Hong Kong

Set ISBN 0-7172-5608-1
Volume ISBN 0-7172-5609-X

Library of Congress Cataloging-in-Publication Data
Science Activities / Grolier Educational
    p. cm.
    Includes index.
    Contents: v.1. Electricity and magnetism—v.2. Everyday Chemistry—v.3. Force and
motion—v.4. Heat and energy—v.5. Inside matter—v.6. Light and color—v.7. Our
Environment—v.8. Sound and hearing—v.9. Using material—v.10. Weather and climate.
ISBN 0-7172-5608-1 (set : alk.paper)—ISBN 0-7172-5609-X (v.1 : alk. paper)—
ISBN 0-7172-5610-3 (v.2 : alk. paper)—ISBN 0-7172-5611-1 (v.3 : alk. paper)—ISBN
0-7172-5612-X (v.4 : alk. paper)—ISBN 0-7172-5613-8 (v.5 : alk. paper)—ISBN
0-7172-5614- 6 (v.6 : alk. paper)—ISBN 0-7172-5615-4 (v.7 : alk. paper)—ISBN
0-7172-5616-2 (v.8 : alk. paper)—ISBN 0-7172-5617-0 (v.9 : alk. paper)—ISBN
0-7172-5618-9 (v.10 : alk. paper)
    1. Science—Study and teaching—Activity programs—Juvenile literature. [1.
Science—Experiments. 2. Experiments] I. Grolier Educational (Firm)

LB1585.S335 2002
507.1'2—dc21
                                                            2001040519

ABOUT THIS SET

Science Activities gives children a chance to explore fascinating topics from the world of science using the same methods that professional scientists use to solve problems. This set introduces young scientists to the scientific method by focusing on the importance of planning experiments, conducting them in a rigorous fashion so that a fair test can be carried out, recording all the stages, and organizing and analyzing the data to draw conclusions. Readers will have the chance to conduct exciting and innovative hands-on activities and to learn how to record and analyze their experiments and results in a variety of ways.

Every volume of *Science Activities* contains 10 step-by-step experiments, along with follow-up activities that encourage readers to find out more about the subject. The activities are explained and enhanced with detailed introductory and analysis sections. Colorful photos illustrate each activity, and every book is packed full of pictures and illustrations explaining the details of each topic.

By working fun and educational experiments into the context of the scientific method, anyone using this set can get a feel for how professional scientists go about their work. Most importantly, just have fun!

PICTURE CREDITS
(b=bottom; t=top)

Corbis: Stuart Calder/(Milepost 92 ½) 4,
Jay Dickman 56, John Francis 49, Lowell
Georgia 38, Richard Hamilton-Smith 19,
David Katzenstein 43, Robert
Kaufman/Yogi, Inc. 61, Danny Lehman 50,
Museum of the City of New York 23,
Vittoriano Rastelli 51, Bob Rowan 28, Paul
A. Souders front cover, 5, Leonard D. Selva
55 (b), Lawson Wood 13 (b), Michael S.
Yamashita 55 (t); **Ecoscene:** Ian Harwood
12; **Genesis Space Photo Library:** 44;
Hulton/Archive: ASAP 37; **Robert
Harding:** Terry Allen/International Stock
29; **Shirreff Thomas/Ace Photo
Agency/Phototake NYC** 33; **Science
Photo Library:** 13 (t), 17, 39, Peter Mezel
27, Sinclair Stammers 45; **Sylvia Cordaiy:**
Chris Parker 6.

CONTENTS

VOLUME 1
ELECTRICITY AND MAGNETISM

INTRODUCTION

During a power cut you can't watch television, play a computer game, or switch on a light. Outside, with no electricity, cars would stop, and all the lights would go out. Electricity truly powers the modern world.

Every substance is made up of tiny invisible particles called atoms. At the center of each atom there are positively charged particles called protons grouped with other particles into a central core called the nucleus. Even smaller particles, called electrons, spin around the nucleus—a little like satellites spinning around Earth. Each electron has a tiny negative charge. An electric charge is a bundle of electrical energy gathered into one place. Everything to do with electricity is ultimately caused by these electrically charged particles.

The way electrons gather in one place, or move from one place to another, causes all the effects associated with electricity. When you switch on a flashlight, electricity flows around the circuit inside. If you could magnify the circuit millions of times, you would see that the electricity is caused by electrons moving around the circuit, carrying little packets of electrical energy.

There are two types of electricity. Static electricity describes what happens when electrical charges remain in one place (static means not moving). A common example of static electricity is the way you can get an electric shock from a door handle after you have walked across a nylon carpet. The other type of electricity, current electricity, describes what

A maglev (magnetic levitation) train is both pushed and pulled along by electromagnets in the rails and on the train. They also make the train float above the rails.

As the girl touches the plasma ball, static electricity flows up to her hair, which stands up because the negative charges (electrons) repel each other.

happens when electrical charges move from one place to another. Current electricity is used in electric and electronic circuits, the connections inside everyday appliances such as video recorders.

ELECTRICITY AND MAGNETISM

Scientists once thought electricity and magnetism were two different forces. The science of electricity explained the behavior of electric charges, while magnetism explained how compasses work and how materials become magnetic. But we now know that electricity produces magnetism, and magnetism produces electricity. That is because electricity and magnetism are two parts of the same force of nature, which physicists today call "electromagnetism."

BE SAFE!

If you have ever watched lightning, you will know that electricity can be very powerful and dangerous. Many people lose their lives by not properly respecting the power of electricity. The experiments in this book are all safe if you follow the instructions very carefully in each one. If you are ever in any doubt about what to do, ask an adult to help you.

The good science guide

Science is not only a collection of facts—it is the process that scientists use to gather information. Follow this good science guide to get the most out of each experiment.

• Carry out each experiment more than once. That prevents accidental mistakes skewing the results. The more times you carry out an experiment, the easier it will be to see if your results are accurate.

• Decide how you will write down your results. You can use a variety of different methods, such as descriptions, diagrams, tables, charts, and graphs. Choose the methods that will make your results easy to read and understand.

• Be sure to write your results down as you are doing the experiment. If one of the results seems very different from the others, it could be because of a problem with the experiment that you should fix immediately.

• Drawing a graph of your results can be very useful because it helps fill in the gaps in your experiment. Imagine, for example, that you plot time along the bottom of the graph and temperature up the side. If you measure the temperature ten times, you can put the results on the graph as dots. Use a ruler to draw a straight line through all the dots. You can now estimate what happened in between each dot, or measurement, by picking any point along the line and reading the time and temperature for that point from the sides of the graph.

• Learn from your mistakes. Some of the most exciting findings in science came from an unexpected result. If your results do not tally with your predictions, try to find out why.

• You should always be careful when carrying out or preparing any experiment, whether it is dangerous or not. Make sure you know the safety rules before you start working.

• Never begin an experiment until you have talked to an adult about what you are going to do.

ACTIVITY 1
BATTERIES AND CELLS

A battery is a handy packet of stored electricity, which can be used to power portable appliances. Most batteries are made up of one or more smaller units called cells. Those cells can be made out of some surprising materials.

B ig appliances such as your refrigerator, television, and computer are powered by the main electricity supply—they are plugged into sockets. If you want to supply power to a small, portable electrical appliance, such as a personal stereo or hand-held computer game, you need portable electricity, which is stored in batteries.

Batteries come in many shapes and sizes, but they all work by storing chemical energy and converting it into electrical energy. This energy then moves around a path made of wires leading from the battery to the item you want to power and back

The bulbs in these holiday lights in London, England, light up because they make a complete circuit.

into the battery. This path is called a circuit. Electricity will flow only if there is a complete path; any break in the circuit will stop the flow of electricity around the path.

Two things are needed to make a circuit work: current and voltage. Current is the size of the flow of electrical energy, carried by electrons, around a circuit. Electrons flow between two points because of the potential difference between the two points.

This potential difference is the voltage, which is measured in volts (V). So, voltage provides the "kick" that sets the electrons flowing. Voltage is also called the electromotive force (emf) because it is the force that sets electricity in motion. Voltage can be measured with a device called a voltmeter.

The basic unit for producing electricity is called a cell. Cells act like pumps, forcing electrons to flow and create electricity. Each kind of cell has a particular voltage. A battery can be made of just one cell or many cells stacked together. Batteries made of just one cell are called single-cell batteries. Each of the 1.5-V batteries in a flashlight is a single cell. The small, pill-shaped batteries that power digital watches are also single cells. Large batteries, like 9-V batteries and car batteries, are made up of many cells stacked together.

The electricity supplied by electrons in a cell or battery always flow from one end, called the negative (−) electrode, or terminal, to the positive (+) end, called the positive electrode, or terminal.

The batteries we use to power portable devices are usually made with several different chemicals, but it is possible to make them using components as simple as some lemons and two pieces of wire, as you will see in the following activity.

How a battery works

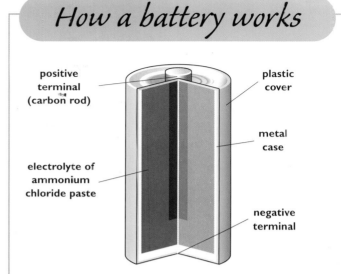

positive terminal (carbon rod)

plastic cover

metal case

electrolyte of ammonium chloride paste

negative terminal

Batteries are a portable source of electric power—they supply the voltage that kicks a circuit into action. Batteries store electrical energy inside them in a chemical form. Gradually, as electricity is produced, the chemicals are turned into other, useless chemicals, and the batteries run down. All batteries have three basic components: a positive electrode (a carbon rod), a negative electrode (made from a different element than the positive electrode), and a chemical called an electrolyte, which separates the terminals and acts as an electron carrier.

Electric circuits

A circuit is the path electricity takes as it flows. There are two main types of circuit: series and parallel. In a series circuit (1 and 2) the parts, such as lightbulbs, are all connected in a single loop. If any connection in the series circuit is broken, no current flows through the circuit at all.

In a parallel circuit (3) each part is connected independently to the power supply. If any one part fails, the others will keep on working.

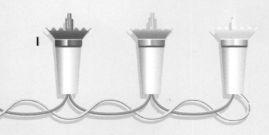

Lights connected in series

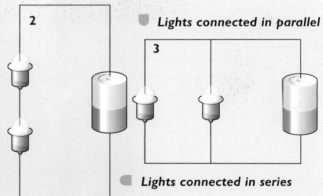

Lights connected in parallel

Lights connected in series

It is useful to connect parts together in series since the current is the same everywhere in this type of circuit. In a parallel circuit the current is shared among the parts. Lights connected in a parallel circuit would burn less brightly because less current powers each one. So, on a string of outdoor lights all the bulbs are connected in series.

Lemon Battery

ACTIVITY

Goals

1. **Use a lemon to build a working battery.**
2. **Explore how electricity flows.**
2. **Test how well your lemon battery works in different conditions.**

What you will need:

- *fresh lemon*
- *stiff copper wire*
- *nail*
- *paper clips*
- *wire clippers*
- *voltmeter or ammeter*
- *zinc-coated screw*
- *electric wires with alligator clips at each end*
- *goggles*

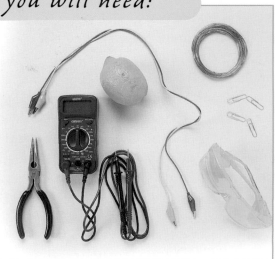

1 Take the lemon, and push on it gently while rolling it along a table top. This releases the juice inside. Take care not to break the skin of the lemon.

Safety tip

The lemon will not generate enough electricity to hurt—but take care when touching your tongue to the wires so that you don't cut yourself.

2 Using the wire clippers, cut a 2-inch (5cm) piece of copper wire. You might want to ask an adult to help you do this. Gently push the wire about 1 inch (2.5cm) into the lemon.

3 Straighten out the paper clip. Gently push the paper clip about 1 inch (2.5cm) into the lemon. Try to get the paper clip as close as you can to the copper electrode without touching it.

Using an ammeter

An ammeter measures current and displays it in amps, and a voltmeter measures voltage and displays it in volts. Ammeters and voltmeters come in two types. Some of them have pointers that swing back and forth across a dial. When a current passes through this type of ammeter, it generates magnetism, which makes the pointer move a bit like a compass needle. Other types of meters have digital displays (like the one we have used in this activity), and they measure current and voltage with electronic circuit boards instead of magnetism.

4 Roll your tongue around your mouth so it is nice and wet. Now, gently touch your tongue to both wire electrodes at the same time. You should feel a slight tingling sensation. Electricity produced by the lemon battery is flowing through your tongue!

Troubleshooting

What if I can't feel a tingling sensation in my tongue?

First, make sure you are using a fresh, moist lemon. You may have to try a couple of different lemons before you get a nice juicy one. Place the wires very close together, and make sure your tongue is moist before touching it to the wires. Sometimes, using thicker copper wire will also make it easier to feel the current.

5 If you have an ammeter or voltmeter, use the electric wires with alligator clips to connect one terminal of the voltmeter to the paper clip and the other terminal to the copper electrode. If the meter shows a negative reading, you have connected your circuit the wrong way around. Swap the connections. Write down the reading in a notebook.

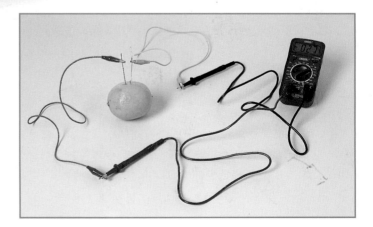

FOLLOW-UP Lemon battery

Take a small lightbulb (rated at around 1.5V) from a flashlight, and connect it to your lemon battery using the alligator clips. Does the bulb light? Probably not. A good lemon battery only produces around 0.5–0.75V, which does not give enough of an electrical "kick" to move electrons through the 1.5-V flashlight bulb.

Multicell lemon battery

To generate more voltage, you could try connecting two or more lemon batteries together in a series. First, make a second lemon battery exactly the same as the first. Then use the alligator clips to connect the steel electrode of one battery to the copper electrode of the other battery. This joins the two batteries together in a series,

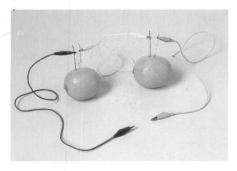

making a multicell lemon battery with a voltage of around 1.0–1.5V. You can connect the two free terminals on the multicell battery to a voltmeter to check the voltage.

Remove the voltmeter, and connect the wires to the flashlight bulb. Does it light?

The multicell lemon battery is now producing up to 1.5V, but remember that voltage is only one of the two things needed to make a circuit work properly. The lemon battery is still only producing a very tiny current. A much bigger current is needed to heat up the filament (the thin wire inside a lamp) to make it glow and give off light. But, you may find that your multicell lemon battery can light an LED display or power a digital watch, because they require only tiny currents.

Fruity batteries

Using the same wire electrodes, repeat the experiment with different fruits. Make a table, and record the voltage from each fruit. You should find that the more acidic the fruit or vegetable, the higher the voltage.

For each fruit repeat the experiment with other pairs of metals. Try one copper electrode and one aluminum electrode (you can use aluminum wrapped around a toothpick to make it stick in the lemon). Or try one copper electrode and one zinc electrode (use a zinc-coated screw). Which electrodes produce the highest voltage?

You can make a cell out of any moist, acidic fruit or vegetable.

Hand battery

If you have a small sheet of copper and a small aluminum sheet (you can buy them from a hardware store), try making this even simpler battery.

Connect one alligator clip from each connection wire to each metal sheet. Connect the other end of the electric wires to your ammeter. To complete the circuit, simply place one hand on each metal sheet. The sweat on your hands acts as an electrolyte and should supply enough electrons to generate a very small current. Does the ammeter show a reading?

ANALYSIS

Batteries and cells

The lemon battery you made in this activity was a single-cell battery. It worked just like the single-cell batteries that power your personal stereo, flashlight, or other portable electric devices.

All cells consist of a liquid, paste, or solid electrolyte, a positive electrode, and a negative electrode. The electrolyte is an acid and acts as a reservoir of electrons. The negative electrode reacts, producing a flow of electrons, while the positive electrode accepts electrons. When the terminals are connected in a circuit, or connected to a device that is going to be powered, the electrons will flow from negative to positive, creating an electrical current.

In your lemon single-cell battery the lemon juice was the electrolyte, the copper wire was the positive electrode, accepting electrons, and the steel paperclip was the negative electrode, producing electrons.

Lemon battery

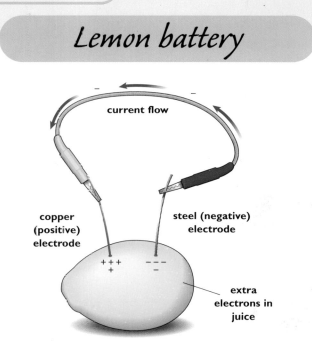

copper (positive) electrode

steel (negative) electrode

current flow

+ + + +

− − − −

extra electrons in juice

The electricity in your lemon cell comes from the flow of electrons around a circuit. The extra electrons gather in the lemon at the end of the paperclip (negative terminal). They flow to the end of the copper wire (positive terminal), where there are fewer electrons. You don't need wire to complete the circuit; you first completed the circuit when you touched the electrodes with your tongue.

When you touched the electrodes with your tongue, or connected a meter to them, the circuit was completed. A chemical reaction took place inside the lemon. Energy from the electrons inside the atoms that make up the lemon juice gathered at the negative electrode and traveled around the circuit to the positive electrode. That was the electric current flowing through the circuit.

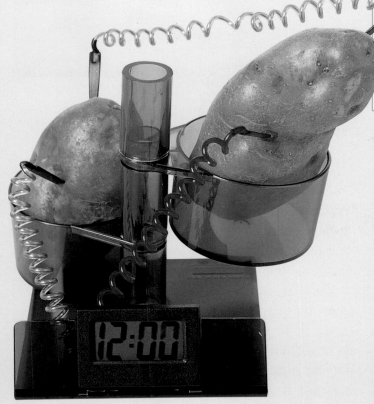

Two potatoes can generate enough electricity to power a small digital clock.

ACTIVITY 2
PILES OF PILES

A single cell on its own does not supply enough electricity to power most electrical devices. To generate enough power, several cells are stacked together into piles of cells all hooked up together. They are called piles.

Electrical cells, like the lemon cell you made in Activity 1 (pages 6 to 11), are the basic units for storing electricity. A 1.5-V battery, like the kind you use in a personal stereo, is a single cell. But as you saw in Activity 1, a single cell does not store a great deal of electricity. That is why most flashlights, personal stereos, and other battery-powered objects use several batteries. The earliest batteries were actually made up of stacks of individual cells. These stacks are called piles.

The first electric cell was, in fact, a pile. It was constructed in 1800 by Italian physicist Alessandro Volta (1745–1827) and was the first source of continuous current. It is sometimes referred to as a voltaic pile (volt and voltage are named after Volta).

Automobile batteries are a type of wet battery. They are called this because they contain liquid sulfuric acid.

Volta's pile was built up like a sandwich, with alternating silver disks (the positive electrodes), cardboard disks soaked in salt water, and zinc disks (the negative electrodes). Volta's pile was an instant sensation because it allowed high-voltage electric currents to be produced for the first time and paved the way for the wider use of electricity.

Volta's experiments were based on the work of another scientist, Italian anatomist Luigi Galvani (1737–1798). Galvani had found that if he hung the leg of a dead frog from an iron hook and then touched it with a different metal, the leg twitched.

Galvani believed the twitching was caused by some kind of "animal" electricity stored inside the frog, but Volta proved otherwise. His experiments showed that it was the two different metals separated by the liquid in the frog's leg that were generating electricity. The frog's leg twitched because electricity was flowing through it, not because it was somehow releasing stored electricity.

A pile is exactly the same thing as a battery, and just like a battery, a pile is made up of numerous different cells. In Volta's pile each sandwich of silver, cardboard soaked in salt water, and zinc is one cell. Just as in your lemon battery, electricity is generated when a pile is connected into a circuit. At that point chemical reactions start to take place in the salt water. Electrons flow through the pile, and an electric current is generated.

MODERN BATTERIES

Using a pile, instead of a single cell, allows a higher voltage to be produced in order to power a wider variety of electric devices. For example, many radios are powered by 9-V batteries, which are made up of six 3-V cells in a pile, and 12-V car batteries contain six 2-V cells in a pile.

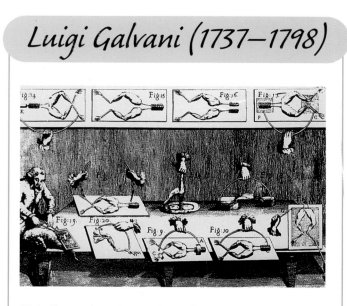

Luigi Galvani (1737–1798)

This illustration shows the different experiments that Luigi Galvani conducted on electricity and frog muscles. In all of these experiments, connecting a frog's leg to two different metals made the muscles in the leg twitch. Galvani believed this happened because there was electricity stored in the muscle. Several years later Alessandro Volta showed that the frog's leg was in fact conducting electricity, not storing it. The engraving above was used to illustrate Galvani's 1791 book *De viribus electricitatis in motu musculari commentarius* (Commentary on Electric Forces in Muscle Movement).

Batteries in which the chemicals are used up are called primary cells. Some batteries can be reused if a current is passed through them in the opposite direction from normal cell operation. These batteries are called secondary cells, or rechargeable batteries. Most batteries used in everyday devices are primary cells. Batteries used in automobiles and other vehicles are secondary cells. They can deliver a strong current of electricity for starting an engine, but they run down quickly and need to be constantly recharged.

In this activity you will make a voltaic pile very much like the first pile built by Volta. Instead of frog legs or silver, yours will be made of coins.

This diver's underwater camera is powered by a single cell, but his flashlight needs a lot more electricity. Several batteries provide the power. Each battery is made of a number of cells in a pile.

Voltaic Pile

Goals

1. **Make your own voltaic pile, based on Alessandro Volta's 1800 model.**
2. **Use pennies and dimes as your electrodes and lemon juice as an electrolyte to make an electric current.**
3. **Measure the current with an ammeter.**

What you will need:

- absorbent paper towel
- scissors
- lemon juice
- 2 plastic plates
- electric wires with alligator clips
- 5–10 copper coins, such as pennies
- the same number of zinc coins, such as dimes
- voltmeter

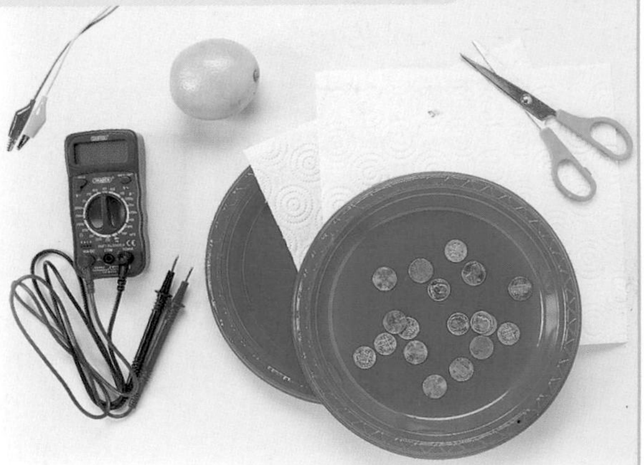

1 Cut the paper towel into pieces about 1 inch (2.5cm) square. You will need between 5 and 10 pieces of paper towel.

2 Soak the pieces of paper towel in lemon juice.

3 Clip one end of an electric wire to one of the pennies. Then build up a sandwich starting with a penny, followed by a piece of lemon-soaked towel, then a dime, then another penny, then another piece of towel, and so on, finishing with a dime. So, between each two towels you have both a penny and a dime. To begin with, just use five of each coin.

4 Connect one end of the second connector wire to the top coin.

Measuring voltage and current

Voltage is measured in units called volts (V). A small battery produces a voltage of around 1.5 V, a lead-acid automobile battery produces around 12 V, and the electricity supply that flows into most households is 110 V.

Current is measured in units called amperes or amps (A), named for French physicist and mathematician André-Marie Ampère (1775–1836). A current of 1 A is really quite large. The currents used in the experiments in this book are typically just a few milliamps—one milliamp is one-thousandth of one amp.

5 Make sure all the layers of the pile are touching. You may have to hold them together by pressing firmly with the alligator clips. Now connect the other ends of the connector wires to the ammeter or voltmeter. If you see no reading on the meter, or the needle moves in a negative direction, change the connections around.

Troubleshooting

What if my pile doesn't work?
The current may not have been flowing through some part of the circuit. First, try cleaning the coins. Then make sure all the parts of the pile are touching one another, and check that all the pieces of paper towel are thoroughly soaked with lemon juice.

6 Repeat the experiment using more coins. In each case record the readings on the ammeter so you can compare them later.

7 If you do not have an ammeter, darken the room completely, and touch the ends of the alligator clips together. You should see a small spark. Does the spark change as you add more coins?

FOLLOW-UP

Voltaic pile

After you have built a pile using coins, you may want to experiment with different metals and materials. Build different piles, and compare the amount of voltage you can generate from each.

Iron nails and zinc screws are cheap and easy-to-find alternative metals for this experiment. They don't stack as easily, but they can be layered (as below). Make sure the paper towels touch both the top and bottom nails.

To understand better how a pile works, try using a pile made entirely of copper coins. You should find that this pile generates no electricity at all.

Instead of using lemon juice, try using other mildly acidic liquids as the electrolyte. Try salt water (dissolve salt in some warm water), vinegar, water, cola, or orange juice. Measure the voltage produced by your pile in each case. Which electrolyte produced the most voltage?

■ *You can also make a pile using zinc screws and iron nails between the towels. Stack the nails carefully so that they don't fall over.*

ANALYSIS

Piles of piles

You might have been surprised to find out just how much electricity you can generate with a few coins and some lemon juice.

The voltage produced by your dime and penny pile should have increased with the number of coins you added. If you were to draw a graph of voltage plotted against the total number of coins used in each pile, it should come out as more or less a straight line.

When you connect a pile into a circuit, for example, by connecting it to an ammeter, a chemical reaction takes place. This reaction occurs where the dimes meet the wet paper towels (electrolyte), and electrons are produced.

Electrons all have a negative charge, and negative charges repel (push away from) one another. As a result, some of the electrons are pushed toward the copper electrode, leaving the zinc

then through the outside circuit (the ammeter), and back into the pile. Any break in the circuit (such as a missing piece of paper towel or two coins not touching) keeps electrons from moving around, so no current will flow. When this happens, we say the circuit is broken or incomplete.

Alessandro Volta's crown of cups was an early battery. It was made up of a series of containers holding salt water and electrodes made from zinc and silver. Metal hoops connected the cells together in a series.

electrode with slightly too few electrons. The copper (penny) electrode becomes negatively charged, and the zinc (dime) electrode becomes positively charged.

Because each zinc electrode in the pile touches the copper electrode next to it, electrons flow through the copper to the zinc. In this way electrons flow through all the parts of the pile,

The pile you made in this activity is put together in the same way as Volta's original pile. Volta also constructed another type of pile using glasses of salty water as the electrolyte and strips of metal as the electrodes.

Volta's pile was one of his later experiments. Earlier in his career Volta invented a device for detecting an electric charge, called an electroscope, which you will have a chance to build in the following activity.

An automobile battery

Most automobiles have a 12-V battery that contains a pile of six 2-V cells. Inside these cells a combination of lead and acid generates electricity. Each cell in the pile contains a lead plate, a lead dioxide plate, and sulfuric acid (a very strong acidic liquid). Unlike dry-cell batteries, in which the electrolyte is a paste, these "wet" cells can be recharged. So, automobile batteries do not have to be replaced as often as flashlight batteries. A lead-acid battery powers the automobile's electrical system. The battery is recharged by power generated as the automobile is running.

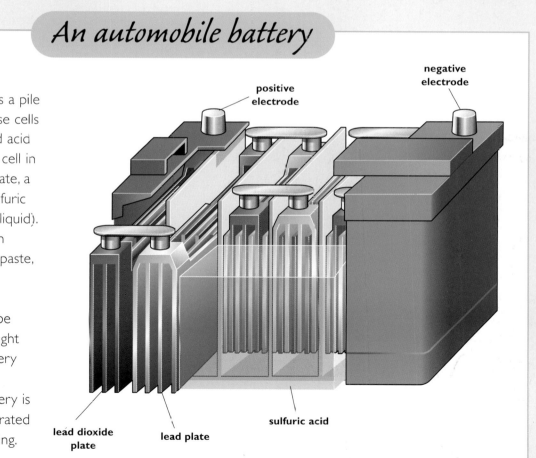

positive electrode

negative electrode

lead dioxide plate

lead plate

sulfuric acid

STATIC ELECTRICITY

Walk across the carpet, reach for the doorknob, and "zap," you get a shock. Come in from the cold, pull off your wool hat, and all your hair stands on end. Both are examples of the unusual effects of static electricity.

Cells and batteries (see Activities 1 and 2) store electric current and move it around a circuit. Electricity that can be made to move around a circuit is called current electricity. Current electricity has been used and understood only since the end of the 18th century. Before that time people only really knew about and understood a kind of electricity that doesn't move in a circuit: static electricity.

STICKY ELECTRICITY

Each atom normally contains the same number of particles called protons and electrons. Protons are positively charged particles, and electrons are negatively charged particles. These particles usually balance each other out. However, sometimes electrons can be removed from atoms. For example, when you rub a balloon on your hair, electrons jump off your hair and onto the balloon. The balloon now has extra electrons. We say that it is charged with static electricity. Because the balloon now has more electrons than protons, it is negatively charged. Your hair, with more protons

than electrons, is now positively charged. The charged balloon will be attracted to anything with either a positive charge or a balanced charge—like your clothes or the wall—and stick to it.

ELECTRON FLOW

So what does all this have to do with shocks or hair that sticks up? When you take off your wool hat, it rubs against your hair. Some electrons move from your hair to the hat. Each of your hairs now has a positive charge (each hair is missing electrons). Since objects with the same charge repel each other, the hairs try to get as far from each other as possible. The farthest they can get is by standing up on your head, away from all the other hairs.

As you walk across a carpet, electrons move from the carpet to your body. Now you have a negative charge (extra electrons). When you touch a doorknob, the electrons jump from you to the knob, and you get a shock.

◗ *These balloons are sticky because they have been charged with static electricity. They are attracted to anything with extra electrons.*

Electricity in the clouds

High up in a cloud, water and ice particles rub against each other and become charged with static electricity. Over time the top of the cloud becomes positively charged (loses electrons), and the bottom of the cloud becomes negatively charged (gains electrons). When the charge difference between the top and bottom of the cloud, or between two nearby clouds, becomes large enough, an electric discharge—a flash of lightning—takes place. At the same time, the negatively charged particles at the bottom of the cloud attract positively charged particles in the ground, and a smaller flash of lightning rises toward the cloud.

Electrons can easily flow through the regular (crystalline) structure of metals, which is why metal wires carry electric currents very efficiently. Materials like this are called conductors because they conduct (carry) electricity.

Spraying static

Crop-spraying airplanes release sprays of fertilizer or insecticide over farmland. To make sure the chemicals aren't blown away, they are given a negative electrical charge. The negatively charged chemical is attracted to the neutral or positively charged plants and soil. So, the chemicals move down to the ground instead of floating around in the air.

Other materials (such as plastic, rubber, clothes, and hair) have atoms joined together in such a way that there are no free electrons to move around and carry a current. This makes them very poor conductors of electricity. Poor conductors are also called insulators because they can insulate (or protect) people from the dangerous effects of electricity. Cables that carry high currents are covered in plastic to keep you from being electrocuted.

Current electricity relies on charge (extra electrons) being able to flow from one place to another through a conductor. Static electricity usually occurs when charge builds up in one place because it cannot flow elsewhere. When you rub a rubber balloon, which is an insulator, the extra electrons (negative charges) stay on the balloon because the plastic and the air that surrounds it are both very poor conductors of electricity.

We usually notice static electricity more in fall and winter when the air is very dry. During the summer the air is more humid. The extra water in the air helps electrons move off more quickly, so objects cannot build up such big charges.

An electroscope is an instrument that shows whether or not an object is charged. In this activity you can build your own electroscope and use it to test how well different objects hold a charge.

Electroscope

Goals

1. **Build an electroscope to show a buildup of electric charge (static electricity).**
2. **Use your electroscope to store static electricity.**

What you will need:

- *glass jar*
- *cardboard*
- *pencil*
- *thick piece of metal wire 5–6 inches (13–15cm) long*
- *thin aluminum foil*
- *tape*
- *plastic comb*

1 Put the jar upside down on top of the cardboard, and draw a circle around the top rim of the jar with a pencil. Cut out the cardboard circle.

Gold-leaf electroscope

An electroscope is a very good instrument for detecting an electric charge. The best electroscopes are made with gold leaf, not aluminum foil. Gold leaf is lighter than aluminum foil, and it conducts electricity better. That makes the electroscope more sensitive and able to detect smaller amounts of static electricity.

2 Bend the wire into a loop, and stick the ends through the cardboard. Make sure the ends stick up about 1 inch (2.5cm) out of the cardboard.

3 Crumple a piece of aluminum foil into a ball, and stick it on top of the wires.

4 Cut a strip of aluminum foil about 4 inches (10cm) long and ½ inch (1cm) wide. Bend the foil in half, and hang it over the wire. Now tape the lid onto the jar. The foil should hang in the center of the jar, away from the glass. If the foil touches the glass, cut it shorter. Don't let the two halves of the foil touch.

5 Rub the plastic comb five to ten times on a sweater or on your hair. Bring the charged comb slowly up to the foil ball on top of your electroscope. The two ends of the foil will rise. The closer the comb, the more they rise.

6 Holding the comb near the foil ball, touch the foil ball briefly with your free hand, and then take that hand away. The two ends of the foil should fall back down to their original position. Slowly move the comb away from the electroscope. You should see the foil rise again and stay there.

FOLLOW-UP Electroscope

Draw marks ¼ inch (0.5cm) apart on a piece of white cardboard.

Remove the cardboard top from your electroscope, and place your cardboard scale in the jar behind the foil strips. Position the scale so that you can clearly read the numbers on the marks behind the foil strips.

Now try charging different objects by rubbing them on a cloth, and use the marks to tell you how high the strips rise. Try rubbing each object five times first, then rub it ten times, and notice how far the strips move.

■ *Use your scale to measure the strength of a number of different electric charges.*

ANALYSIS
Static electricity

When you rubbed the plastic comb, it became positively charged (lost electrons). When you brought the comb up to the foil ball, the positively charged comb "pulled" electrons from the foil toward it. Because the metal foil was touching the metal wire and also the foil strip, electrons were dragged up through the foil strip and the wire toward the foil ball, giving it a negative charge. But as the electrons left the two ends of the foil, they became positively charged. The two pieces of foil then both had positive charges and pushed away from each other (because like charges repel).

■ *Negative charges are drawn up to the foil ball by the positive charges on the comb. The two foil strips are now both positively charged and fly apart.*

When you touched the foil ball, its negative charge flowed through your body to the ground. This is called grounding (or sometimes "earthing") the charge. Earth is such a big object that it can never be charged, and it will instantly soak up any electric charge in contact with it. When you grounded the ball by touching it, the foil strip collapsed because electrons rushed into the ball from the Earth and canceled out the positive charges on the foil. When you took away the comb, some extra electrons from the comb remained behind and made the foil strips spring apart again.

ACTIVITY 4
LIGHTNING IN A JAR

When lightning strikes, it can set buildings on fire and cause serious injury. But lightning doesn't only come in huge bolts from the clouds. You can make tiny bolts of lightning using a small amount of static electricity.

Before Volta's invention of the pile (see pages 12 to 17), and the understanding of current electricity, scientists looked for ways to store static electricity. One early device for storing static electricity was called the Leyden jar.

The Leyden jar was invented in 1745 by E. Georg von Kleist (1700–1748) at the University of Leyden in the Netherlands. His Leyden jar was a glass jar with a metal coating on both the inside and outside. This combination of two conductors (the metal coatings) separated by an insulator (the glass) was an efficient way to store charge. The jars were charged with static electricity by touching a metal knob on the outside of the jar to a source of static electricity.

Benjamin Franklin (1706–1790) carried out a famous experiment in 1752, and most people know it involved flying a kite in a storm. But many people do not know that Franklin was attempting to store the electricity from the cloud in a Leyden jar.

When a storm cloud passed over Franklin's kite, the negative charges in the cloud leaked onto the kite, down the kite string, a key, and into a Leyden jar attached to the key by a thin metal wire. Franklin was unaffected by the negative charges because he was holding a dry silk string that insulated him from the charges on the key.

Franklin successfully stored the electric charge from a cloud in a Leyden jar during his famous experiment. You can see the Leyden jar in the engraving above.

Today, we often use a device called a capacitor to store electric charge. Small capacitors are used in televisions and computers. Capacitors are made of thin metal plates separated by thin layers of plastic. Connecting wires are welded to the metal plates.

A capacitor works a bit like a water tower. A water tower "stores" water pressure—when there is more water than a town needs, the excess is stored in the water tower. At times of high demand the excess water flows out of the tower to keep the pressure up. A capacitor stores electrons in the same way and can release them later.

Having a way to store electric charge was a big step forward for the 18th-century scientists exploring electricity. In this activity you will have a chance to duplicate their work by building your own Leyden jar, storing an electric charge, and using it to make a miniature bolt of lightning.

ACTIVITY

Leyden Jar

Goals

1. **Build a Leyden jar.**
2. **Store electricity in your Leyden jar.**
3. **Create a small bolt of lightning.**

What you will need:

- *plastic container with a lid*
- *aluminum foil*
- *white glue*
- *metal screw*
- *metal cabinet knob*
- *copper wire*
- *thin wire, such as piano wire*
- *wire cutters*
- *1-foot (30cm) PVC pipe*
- *cotton cloth*

1 Tear or cut a strip of aluminum foil about two-thirds as tall as the plastic container and big enough to wrap around the inside once. The foil must be very smooth. Glue the foil to the inside of the container so it attaches tightly to the plastic.

3 Ask an adult to help you push the screw halfway through the plastic lid, with the head of the screw on the inside. The pointed end of the screw should stick out of the plastic far enough to screw the cabinet knob onto it. Cut a piece of copper wire about 6 inches (15cm) long, and wrap one end of the wire around the screw. Tape the other end of the wire to the foil on the inside of the container.

Safety tip

Do not use flammable glue (such as rubber cement) to stick the foil down because it might catch fire. Ask an adult to help you chose which type of glue to use. You can also use non-flammable wax or tape.

2 Glue an identical strip of foil around the outside of the plastic container.

4 Put the lid on the container. Cut three pieces of thin wire, each about 3 inches (7.5cm) long. Wrap one end of each wire around the screw close to the plastic. Screw the cabinet knob onto the pointed end of the screw. The short wires should stick out past the cabinet knob.

5 Tape another 6-inch (7.5cm) copper wire to the outside foil. Leave one end of this wire free, but make sure it is touching the table.

6 Rub the PVC pipe with the cloth. After several seconds lightly touch the pipe to the short wire sticking out from under the knob on the top of the jar. Repeat this step at least five times to charge your Leyden jar.

Troubleshooting

What if I don't get a spark?
You may not have charged the jar enough. Try repeating step 6 five or ten more times.

On a humid (moist) day the air conducts electricity much better. This means that electric charge may leak out of your jar through the air as quickly as you put it in. Try to do the experiment on a dry day.

Electric charges tend to gather and leak away at sharp points. That is why it is important not to have any creases in your foil. Also, make sure the foil is attached to the plastic container as tightly as possible.

Safety tip

Although it is fun to make sparks, it can be dangerous. The bigger the spark, the higher the voltage. Large Leyden jars are big enough to store dangerous voltages, so use only a small container. Never fool around with electricity.

7 Put down the pipe, and pick up the free end of the wire taped to the outside foil. Slowly bring the free end of the wire to the knob. Look closely. A tiny spark should fly across the gap between the wire and the screw.

FOLLOW-UP Leyden jar

The length of the spark you make tells you how big a voltage you have stored in your jar. An easy way to increase the charge you give to your jar is by increasing the number of times you rub the PVC pipe and then touch the pipe to the wires. Be careful when doing this, since you can get a shock if you charge the jar too much.

Leyden jars can be made in a variety of sizes and shapes. It is best to use curved jars, rather than square ones, because the charge tends to leak out where the foil is creased or has edges.

However, a Leyden jar can be made out of any size container. An empty film canister makes a very good, very portable Leyden jar.

Experiment further by building Leyden jars out of larger and smaller containers. What effect does this have on the size of your sparks?

In general, the larger the jar, the larger the area of foil for storing charge, and the larger the spark that can be generated.

ANALYSIS
Lightning in a jar

The PVC pipe is an insulator, so charge does not flow through it easily. Because of this, when you rubbed the pipe, electrons came off the cloth, and a negative static charge (extra electrons) built up on the pipe. The thin metal wires on the container are good conductors. When you touched the pipe to the wires, the charge moves from the pipe, through the wires, down the screw and the inside wire, and onto the foil inside the container.

Once inside the container, the charge had nowhere to go. The plastic container is also an insulator, and the negative charge was trapped on the inner foil.

When the long wire on the outside of the container was touching the table, it is said to be grounding the charge. As long as this wire is touching the table, the positive charge on the outer foil also had nowhere to go—it was grounded. So, a negative charge built up inside the container, separated from the positive charge on the outside of the container.

When you brought the wire from the outside of the container to the knob, the voltage you created in the jar was large enough to make the opposite charges attract. The spark was electrons leaping over the gap and flowing from the negatively charged inner foil to the positively charged outer foil. This canceled out the charges on both pieces of foil with what is called a static discharge. That discharge was the spark that you saw.

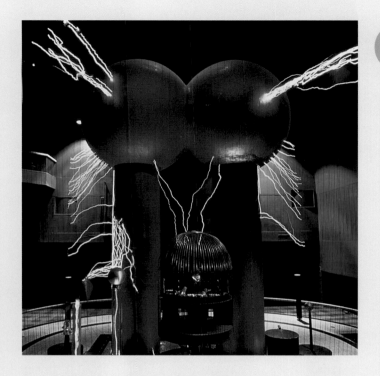

The device above is a Van de Graff generator built in 1931 by U.S. scientist Robert Jemison Van de Graff (1901–1967). It acts like a large Leyden jar to produce 2.5 million volts. The person inside is sitting in a Faraday cage, a device that protects against electric discharge.

Air is normally a very good insulator; but when there is a high enough voltage, air will conduct electricity. A lightning storm is an example of this. A spark or flash of lightning indicates that electricity is flowing through the air. The bigger the spark, the greater the voltage. Roughly 25,000V are needed to make a spark 1 inch (2.5cm) long (or 10,000V for a 1-cm spark). Thus it takes 2,500V to make a spark $\frac{1}{10}$ inch (2.5mm) long.

A bolt of lightning works in the same way as your Leyden jar but carries much more voltage. It takes about 100 million volts in a cloud to create a single bolt of lightning. That is what makes lightning strikes so dangerous. With your Leyden jar you are creating safe, miniature bolts of lightning.

Following the invention of the Leyden jar, scientists began experimenting with the stored charge. These experiments helped pave the way for the creation of motors and generators, and for the many ways we use electric power today.

How a Leyden jar works

The Leyden jar below is another design you could build. This jar has a chain instead of a wire that conducts charge to the inside of a glass jar. The jar is charged by touching a source of static electricity (PVC pipe) to the knob on the top. Negative charge builds up on the inner foil, and positive charge builds up on the outer foil. While the jar is grounded, nothing happens. But when the grounding wire is brought up to the knob, the positive charge on the outer foil flows up the wire. At the same time, negative charge flows from the inner foil up the chain and to the knob. The two opposite charges attract each other, and a spark is created.

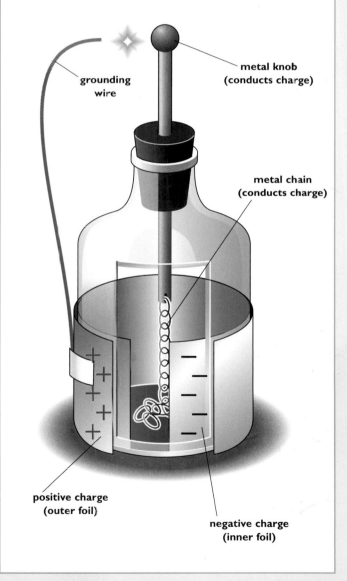

grounding wire

metal knob (conducts charge)

metal chain (conducts charge)

positive charge (outer foil)

negative charge (inner foil)

ACTIVITY 5
INTERRUPTED CURRENT

Why don't birds sitting on overhead wires get electrocuted?
Because they are poor conductors compared to the metal wires that they
are sitting on, so the electricity flows more easily through the wire.

The property that distinguishes a good conductor from a poor conductor is called resistance. The resistance of a material is a measurement of how little electricity it conducts. Because of its structure an insulator, such as plastic, has a very high resistance—it resists electrons trying to flow through it. But a good conductor such as a metal puts up little resistance when electrons try to flow through it. Resistance is the opposite of conductance: A good conductor (such as copper used for wiring) has low resistance, while a poor conductor (such as plastic, used to coat wiring) has high resistance.

Resistance is also a way of relating the voltage that is applied to a circuit to the current that flows through the circuit. If you put a certain voltage (measured in volts) across a piece of plastic, and a very tiny current (measured in amps) flows through it, the resistance is clearly quite high. But if you put the same voltage across a metal, and a much higher current flows, the resistance must be low. In other

Circuit breakers at a power substation automatically flick off a switch to interrupt the power supply when there is a fault.

words, for a given voltage the amount of current that flows depends on the resistance of the circuit. This is known as Ohm's law, named for the German physicist Georg Simon Ohm (1789–1854), who discovered it. Resistance is measured in units called ohms. One ohm of resistance means that one volt is required to keep a current of one amp flowing.

WHY RESISTANCE MEANS HEAT

When electrons flow through a material, some of them collide with the atoms that make up the material. An electron has energy while it is speeding along, but after it collides with an atom, some of that energy is captured by the atom it collides with. The atoms in all materials vibrate back and forth. If an electron collides with one of them, the atom vibrates faster—it heats up.

HOW FUSES WORK

Electrons flow more easily through thick wires than through thin ones. In a thick wire most electrons can flow freely, and there are relatively few collisions between electrons and atoms, so the wire does not heat up much. Most of the electricity flows through the wire, so it has very little resistance. But in very thin wire fewer electrons flow straight through, and there are more collisions. Thin wire heats up more and has a higher resistance than thick wire of the same material.

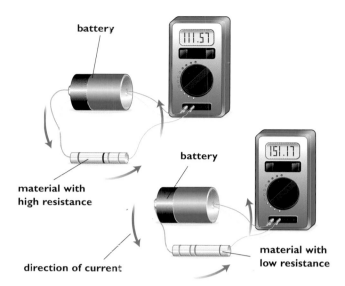

The voltage sent out by the battery in both cases is the same, but a more powerful resistor means that less current reaches the ammeter.

Electrical and electronic equipment can be damaged by big surges of current, which sometimes happen when power plants have trouble regulating their output. Many appliances contain a fuse. The fuse consists of a very thin piece of wire able to carry only a certain amount of current. For example, a 3-amp fuse, which is the kind used in everyday household plugs, can carry a current of 3 amps. If a larger current flows, the wire heats up so much that it burns through and breaks the circuit, protecting the appliance from damage. When the circuit is broken, circuit breakers flip a switch and turn the current off, protecting the electric supply.

Lamps and heat

Household lamps work by getting hot when current flows through them. Inside a glass lightbulb, there is a coil of very fine wire called a filament. When electric current flows through the filament, it glows red hot and gives off light. Lamps also give off a lot of heat. In fact, about 90 percent of the energy lightbulbs give off is heat, and only 10 percent is light, so they are actually more efficient heaters than lamps! That is why lamps are used to keep chicks warm in artificial incubators (right).

Fitting a Fuse

Goals

1. **Make your own fuse.**
2. **Compare different fuse materials in an electric circuit.**

What you will need:

- *very fine iron wire (such as piano wire)*
- *copper wire*
- *4 electric connector leads with alligator clips at both ends*
- *6-volt or 12-volt battery*
- *ammeter (optional)*

Safety tip

A fuse gets hot and burns through when too much current flows through it. If you see the iron wire fuse in your circuit glowing red hot, that means its temperature is very hot. Do not be tempted to touch the iron wire at any time when the battery is connected. It could give you a burn. Wait several minutes for the wire to cool down before you handle it. Always conduct this activity on a nonflammable surface.

1 Cut a 2-inch (5cm) length of copper wire and the same length iron wire. Twist the two together at one end to make a longer wire.

2 Take a lead, and attach one alligator clip to the free end of the very fine iron wire. Attach the other end of the lead to one terminal of the battery.

3 Clip a second lead onto the free end of the copper wire.

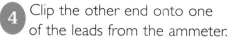

4 Clip the other end onto one of the leads from the ammeter.

5 Take a third lead with alligator clips. Attach one alligator clip to the other ammeter lead.

7 Look at the ammeter. You should find the current has increased. Look again at the fine iron wire. Do you see anything happening?

8 Keep repeating steps 6 and 7 until you notice the iron wire starting to glow red hot. Eventually, it will burn through and break completely. Note the reading on the ammeter when this happens.

6 Clip the second alligator clip to the other terminal of the battery. If the ammeter needle flicks the wrong way or does not move, try switching the battery terminal leads. Look closely at the fine iron wire. Does it break? Do not touch the iron wire with your fingers because it could be hot. If the iron wire has not broken, carefully move the alligator clips between the iron and copper wires to shorten the iron wire. Shorten the wire until it breaks.

FOLLOW-UP · Fitting a fuse

Look at fuse wires rated for different current values. What do you notice about the wire as the current rating increases? Is a piece of 2-amp fuse wire thicker or thinner than a piece of 5-amp fuse wire?

Try a number of different fuse wires in place of the fine iron wire in your circuit. Test the point at which each wire burns out. Make a table, and for each wire write down the approximate length of the wire when it breaks and the current that the ammeter displays just before the fuse burns through. See if this tallies with the current rating of each type of fuse wire and its thickness. For example, a 2-amp fuse wire should burn out at a lower current than a 5-amp fuse wire. Remember to allow the wire to cool before you touch it.

See if you can find some cartridge fuses (like the one shown on the right). With the help of an adult, try cutting open a cartridge fuse to look inside.

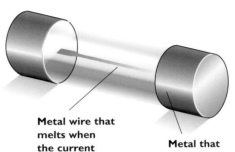

Metal wire that melts when the current rises above a certain level.

Metal that connects the fuse to a circuit.

Fuses such as this one are fitted in plugs that you have around the house. A plug and its lead link electrical appliances, such as the radio or television, to a current.

ANALYSIS

Interrupted current

The copper wire in your circuit does not burn out. That is because copper is a good electrical conductor. In your circuit the piece of iron wire is the fuse. As the current increases, the fine iron wire gets hotter. Eventually, it will get so hot that it burns through and breaks.

As you shortened the iron wire, you should have noticed that the current increased. This happens because the resistance of a wire increases with its length. The longer a piece of wire, the farther electrons have to travel, and the more atoms in the wire they bump into on the way. Shortening the iron wire reduces the distance the electrons have to travel and the resistance they meet. The voltage across the circuit stays the same because you are using the same battery. So if the resistance is decreasing, the current flowing through the circuit increases each time you shorten the wire.

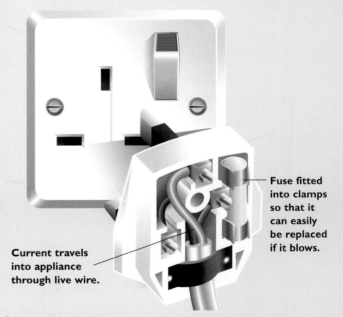

Fuse fitted into clamps so that it can easily be replaced if it blows.

Current travels into appliance through live wire.

The household current flows through the live pin of this 220V plug and then through the fuse. The fuse will melt if there is a damaging power surge.

ACTIVITY 6
DEMAGNETIZE

We think of magnetism in a metal as a permanent force that is always in the metal, but all metals can be demagnetized by heating them up to their Curie point—the temperature at which they lose their magnetic properties.

A magnet sends out an invisible force of attraction all around it called a magnetic field. We think of magnets as attracting, but all magnets both attract and repel. Every magnet has both a north pole and a south pole, which are attracted to Earth's North and South poles, respectively. The north poles of two magnets push away from (repel) each other, while the north pole of one magnet attracts the south pole of another.

Some materials, like iron and steel, are not normally magnetic, but can be made into magnets. In these materials the electrons inside the atoms act like tiny magnets themselves. A number of these electron "magnets" will join to form larger areas of magnetism called magnetic domains. When the material is not magnetized, its domains are all jumbled up, and the little electron magnets point in random directions.

When a small amount of magnetism is applied to the material (for example, when a magnet is brought close to a piece of iron), some of the domains will turn to face the same direction. The iron has

These magnets attract different amounts of iron filings according to their strength. The strongest magnets pull filings away from the weaker magnets.

become a temporary magnet, but its magnetism disappears when the magnet is taken away. If more magnetism is applied (for example, by rubbing the iron with a magnet), the domains all turn to face the same direction and remain there. The iron has become a permanent magnet. The atoms in substances like wood and plastic do not form domains, so they cannot be magnetized.

Just as the domains in iron can be made to line up to create a magnet, they can also be jumbled up again to demagnetize the iron. There are different ways of doing this. One way is to hit a magnet a number of times. The vibrations travel through the crystal structure and jumble up the domains, removing the overall magnetism.

Another way to remove magnetism is with heat. Above a certain temperature vibrations in the material are so great that domains cannot line up to make an effective magnet. This temperature is called the Curie point, and it is different for every material. You can measure the Curie point in the activity on the following pages.

Curie Point

Goals

1. **Heat a paper clip to its Curie point.**
2. **Use heat to remove magnetism from a material.**

What you will need:

- *2 tripods or stands*
- *strong, round magnet*
- *string*
- *paper clip*
- *6-V battery*
- *connection wires with alligator clips*

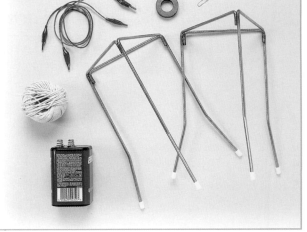

1 Suspend the magnet on a piece of string from one of the tripods.

2 Use string to tie the paper clip between two legs of the second tripod. The paper clip should be at the same height as the magnet.

3 Move the tripods closer together until the magnet attracts the paper clip and sticks to it.

4 Clip one connection lead to each end of the paper clip. Now attach the remaining ends of the connection wires to the two terminals of the battery. It does not matter which way around you connect them.

5 As the paper clip heats up, the magnet should fall away from the paper clip. The paper clip might be hot at this point, so do not touch it.

Why is Earth magnetic?

The molten iron inside Earth's core is hotter than its Curie point, yet the Earth is magnetic. No one knows why. One theory is that electric currents circulate inside Earth's liquid core and create a magnetic field as they move.

FOLLOW-UP Curie point

Once the magnet has fallen away, disconnect the battery, and allow some time for the paper clip to cool down. Do not be tempted to touch it while it is still hot—you should wait about five minutes.

When the paper clip has cooled, bring the magnet up to it once more. You should find that the magnet and the paper clip will attract each other and stick together again.

You may also want to repeat the experiment using a different metal. Iron nails or thin iron wire also work very well.

There are other ways to demagnetize temporary magnets. Magnetize an iron nail by stroking it with a permanent magnet, moving the magnet only in one direction. Some of the domains will now be pointing in the same direction. Check that the nail is magnetic by touching it to a paper clip and making sure they stick together.

Take a hammer and, placing the nail on the pavement or a hard work surface, give the nail a few taps with the

hammer (always check with an adult before doing this!). Striking the nail with the hammer should scramble up the domains, demagnetizing the nail. Check this by touching it to the paper clip again.

ANALYSIS
Demagnetize

You should have found that the magnet falls away from the paper clip a short time after you connect the battery. As the current runs through the metal, it heats up. When the metal in the clip heats up to its Curie point, its magnetic domains jumble up. Once this happens, the paper clip no longer has a magnetic field, and the magnet falls away. As soon as the metal cools off to a temperature below its Curie point, it becomes magnetic again, and the magnet will stick to it.

Not all materials, or even all metals, can become permanent magnets when they are placed next to another magnet. Materials that can become permanent magnets are called ferromagnets. Iron, cobalt, nickel, gadolinium, and dysprosium are the only ferromagnetic

elements, although many alloys and compounds (mixtures of two or more elements) are also ferromagnets.

Paper clips are usually made from steel, which is an alloy of iron and carbon. A paper clip should contain enough iron to become magnetized and attracted to the magnet. If it is not attracted to the magnet, then the paper clip is probably made of another material, and you should use thin iron wire instead.

MARIE AND PIERRE CURIE

The Curie point is named for French physicist Pierre Curie (1859–1906). Although most famous for his work on radioactivity, which he conducted with his wife, Marie Curie

(1867–1934), and for which they shared a Nobel Prize in 1903 with Henri Becquerel (1852–1908), Pierre Curie also conducted extensive research into magnetism.

Pierre Curie discovered the Curie point, the temperature below which a ferromagnetic material becomes magnetic, in 1895. He later formulated Curie's law, which describes how the magnetic attraction of materials changes with temperature and disappears at the Curie point. Pierre Curie also discovered piezoelectricity, the way some materials generate electricity when under pressure.

▶ *French scientists Marie and Pierre Curie (shown here) are most famous for their work on radioactivity, for which they shared a Nobel Prize for Chemistry in 1903. Their daughter, Irene Joliot-Curie (1897–1956), won the Nobel Prize for Chemistry in 1935.*

Continental drift and plate tectonics

| 300 million years ago | 200 million years ago | 150 million years ago | Today | 50 million years in the future? |

Since at least the early 17th century people have noticed that many of the world's coastlines, like those of West Africa and eastern South America, seem to fit together like a giant jigsaw puzzle. Geologists now believe that the continents are huge plates of land that rest on liquid rock deep within the Earth. Scientists believe that hundreds of millions of years ago the continents were one big landmass and have been slowly moving apart. This theory is called plate tectonics. Proof for the theory came from studying the magnetic fields of rock containing iron. When molten iron rock (magma) erupts from deep inside the Earth,

its temperature is far above the Curie point for iron, so it is not magnetic. But as the rock cools down below its Curie point, the magnetic domains in the rock line up with Earth's magnetic field—revealing the direction of Earth's poles from the rock at that time.

Magma tends to erupt where the continental plates meet, pushing the continents apart. By studying the magnetic fields of the rock on the ocean floor and on the continents, geologists have been able to put together a map of where the continents were at different times in Earth's history and to prove that the continents do indeed move apart over time.

MOTORING ON

Electric motors are the workhorses of the modern world—clean, quiet, and powerful. The secret of their operation is the interaction between electric currents and magnetic fields.

The electric motor is one of the most important modern inventions. Many different types and sizes of electric motors are used all around us. Most motors are very efficient and do not cause much pollution. Large, powerful motors can be used anywhere electric power cables can reach, while smaller and less powerful ones can be run on batteries.

Electric motors depend on electromagnetism—magnetism generated by electric currents. In Activity 9 (pages 52 to 53) you can make an electromagnet using only a coil of wire and a battery. Just like an ordinary bar magnet, an electromagnet has a north pole and a south pole.

Just as two ordinary magnets attract or repel one another, two electromagnets, or one ordinary magnet and one electromagnet, do the same thing. Hold a bar magnet down on a table, and slide

This robotic Mars explorer is being tested on Earth. It has powerful, compact electric motors to drive its wheels. The motors do not need oxygen or a heat supply but are powered by an onboard nuclear generator.

another magnet up close to it. You will feel a force acting on the two magnets—pushing them apart if the two poles closest to each other are the same, or pulling them together if they are different. If you release the second magnet, it will move toward or away from the first one. Magnetism can make things move.

Now imagine that the fixed magnet is an electromagnet, and the movable magnet is an ordinary bar magnet. With no current the electromagnet has no magnetic field, and there is no magnetic force acting on either of the magnets. Once you switch the current on, however, the electromagnet either attracts or repels the ordinary magnet.

You can also set up the electromagnet so that it does not move in a straight line, but instead spins around. Suppose the north pole of the bar magnet is the pole that is closest to the electromagnet; the electromagnet will now turn until its south pole is closer to the bar magnet. The electromagnet might swing back and forth for a while, but it would eventually settle down with its south pole as close as possible to the bar magnet's north pole.

If you reversed the current through the electromagnet, its north and south poles would change places. The new north pole would be next to the bar magnet's north pole and would be pushed away. The electromagnet would spin around. If you kept switching the current, constantly flipping the electromagnet's poles, the electromagnet would keep spinning. The motor would keep working for as long as current was supplied to it.

HOW ELECTRIC MOTORS WORK

This is the basic idea behind an electric motor, a machine that converts electrical energy into mechanical energy. The motor usually contains permanent magnets or electromagnets that produce a fixed magnetic field. There is also a rotor, which is an electromagnet that spins because of the effect of the fixed magnetic field. The current in the rotor is continually and automatically reversed so that the rotor never settles down in one position.

Bar magnet

When two bar magnets are brought close together, they repel each other (push each other apart) if the two closer poles are the same (below, top). The magnets attract each other if the two closer poles are different (below, bottom). The field lines show the magnetic forces between the two magnets. An electric motor works because inside it there are magnetic fields pushing and pulling each other.

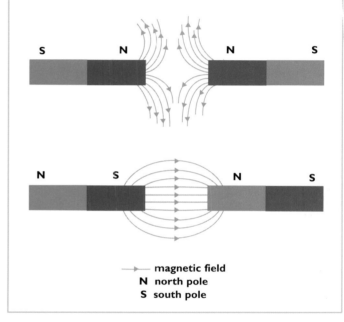

→ **magnetic field**
N north pole
S south pole

The first motors

The electric motor started with the work of 19th-century physicists who showed that electricity and magnetism are really the same force. A Danish physicist, Hans Christian Oersted (1777–1851), discovered that an electric current can produce a magnetic field. His experiment is described in Activity 9 on page 50. André-Marie Ampère (1775–1836), a French physicist, worked out a mathematical theory that describes how a current generates a magnetic field. The unit of current, the amp, is named for him. Later, a self-taught British chemist and physicist, Michael Faraday (1791–1867), proved that when magnetic fields vary in strength, they can produce electricity.

Electric motors were developed after two scientists had built the first practical working electromagnets. They were Joseph Henry (1797–1878) in the United States and William Sturgeon (1783–1850) in Great Britain. It was Sturgeon (below) who produced the first working electric motor, in 1832. The key to Sturgeon's invention was a device called a commutator, which constantly reversed the current supplied to the electromagnet. Most of the electric motors used today are still based on Sturgeon's original design.

Motor Effect

Goals

1. **Make a simple electric motor, and use it to move a wire.**

2. **Use Fleming's left-hand rule to predict the direction of movement of your motor.**

What you will need:

- *large, firm wooden board*
- *strong tape*
- *two 1.5-V batteries*
- *two powerful bar magnets*
- *thin wire, such as piano wire*
- *two electrical wires with alligator clips at each end*

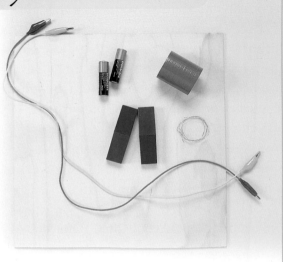

1 Tape the two batteries to the board so that they are in a series—the positive terminal of one touches the negative terminal of the other. The two are now equivalent to one 3-V battery.

2 Tape the two bar magnets firmly to the board with a small gap of about ½ inch (1cm) between them. The north pole of one magnet should face the south pole of the other.

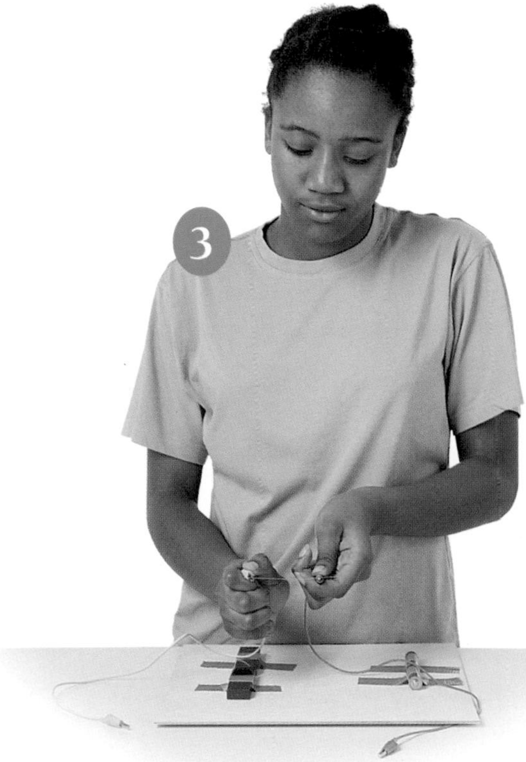

3 Cut a piece of wire about 2 inches (5cm) long. Clip one lead to each end of the wire. Place the wire between the two bar magnets. Make sure the wire is in the middle of the gap.

Troubleshooting

How can I make the wire move by a larger amount?

Make sure the magnets are correctly positioned. The poles that face each other need to be of opposite kinds—one north-seeking, the other south-seeking. This ensures that the field is as strong as it can be and is at right angles to the wire. That will produce the strongest possible magnetic force to pull on the wire.

4 Touch the other ends of the leads to the battery terminals. Watch the wire carefully—it should move a little.

5 Try reversing the leads so that each one touches the other terminal of the batteries. Which way does the wire move?

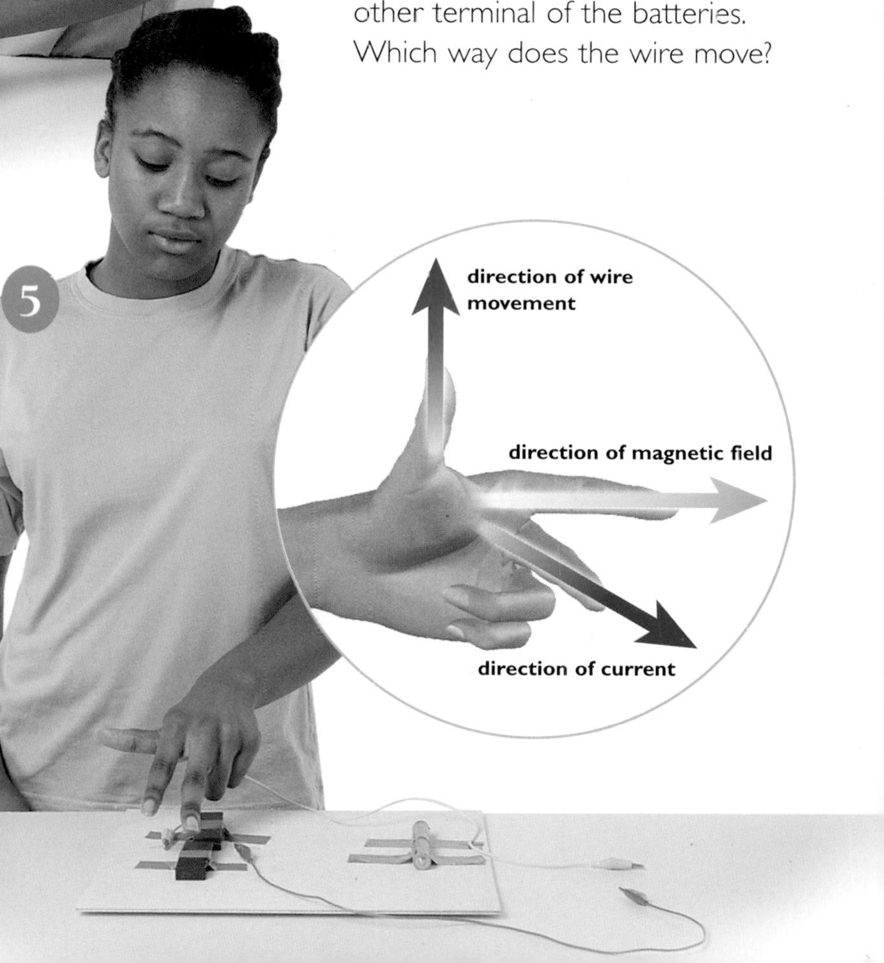

Fleming's left-hand rule

To predict which way the wire will move, use Fleming's left-hand rule. Hold your left hand with the thumb, first, and second fingers at right angles. Point your first finger in the direction of the magnetic field (from north to south; look at the diagrams on page 39). Point your second finger in the direction of the current flow. Your thumb shows the direction of wire movement.

direction of wire movement

direction of magnetic field

direction of current

FOLLOW-UP   Motor effect

Switch the magnets around so that the direction of the magnetic field across the gap is reversed. What effect does this have on the movement of the wire when you switch on the current? Is it what you would expect from Fleming's left-hand rule? (Remember that you now have to point your first finger in the opposite direction.)

Touch each lead to the other battery terminal to reverse the current. Notice the effect this has on the direction of movement of the wire.

Try increasing the strength of the magnetic field by using stronger magnets, or use more magnets. You can also increase the current by using four 1.5-V batteries instead of two. What effects do these changes have?

Making a generator

Electric motors and all other electric devices would be useless without a supply of electricity. Most electricity is made by devices called generators, which are like electric motors working in reverse. In a motor electricity makes a part called the rotor turn, but in a generator a revolving rotor produces electricity.

1. Remove the batteries from your setup. Connect an ammeter (current meter) in their place (left).

2. If you do not have an ammeter, use a small magnetic compass as a current detector. Electric currents are surrounded by magnetic fields, so they affect compasses. Connect the two free alligator clips to each other. Put the compass near them, but not near the bar magnets.

3. Take the wire running between the permanent magnets in your fingers, and lift it sharply through the magnetic field. Watch the ammeter (or compass) as you do this. Does the needle twitch as you move the wire?

4. Now move the wire the opposite way between the magnets. Again, watch the movement of the ammeter or compass. Does the needle move the opposite way?

Moving the wire in the magnetic field generates a brief electric current. You have just made some electricity!

ANALYSIS
Motoring on

When you connect the battery one way, the wire should move a little, either up or down. When you reverse the current (by switching the connections on the battery), the wire should twitch in the opposite direction, as predicted by Fleming's left-hand rule.

Connecting the battery makes a current flow through the wire, and that produces a magnetic field all around the wire. It turns the wire into an electromagnet, although a much weaker one than the electromagnet that you make by coiling a wire around a nail in Activity 9 on pages 52 to 53. While the wire is acting as an electromagnet, it attracts or repels the bar magnets, and that makes the wire jump.

If you made the generator in the follow-up activity, you demonstrated the reverse effect from making a motor in the main activity.

end up with quite a list—from fans, microwave ovens, and electric toothbrushes, to vacuum cleaners, personal computers, and power drills. Think about how motors drive these appliances. A motor drives the fan in a vacuum cleaner. The speed of the motor can be adjusted to alter the vacuum's suction power so that it can be used to clean different surfaces.

Although nearly all automobiles are powered by gasoline engines, even they contain additional small electric motors to power the windshield wipers, cassette and CD players, air conditioning, and windows.

Most of the motors we use every day work in exactly the same way; the main difference between them is in their size and power. A much larger, and stronger, motor is needed to rotate a washing machine drum full of wet clothes than to pull a length of magnetic tape through a personal stereo.

Electric motors come in all sizes. The motor that powers this toy is small, but it works in the same way as the much larger motors used in bigger devices.

Whenever a conductor moves in a magnetic field, electricity flows. The wire is a conductor; and as you moved it through the magnetic field, electricity was generated. It was only a very small amount of electricity, but it should have been strong enough to affect the ammeter or compass needle.

The modern world depends on electric motors. In factories most of the heavy machinery is operated by electric motors. So is machinery in office and apartment blocks, such as air-conditioning units and the motors that haul elevators up and down. Smaller motors open and close automatic doors.

Electric motors are just as important in the home. Take a few minutes to go around your house, making a list of all the appliances you can find that use electric motors. You should

Fleming's right-hand rule

The direction of the electric current produced by a generator can be found using Fleming's right-hand rule. Hold your right hand in the same position as for the left-hand rule, and point your first finger in the direction of the magnetic field. Point your thumb in the direction of movement of the wire that carries the current. Your second finger shows the direction of the current.

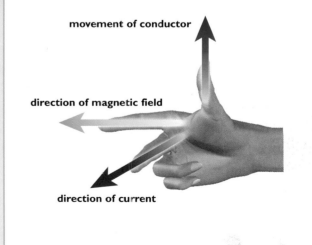

movement of conductor

direction of magnetic field

direction of current

ACTIVITY 8
MAGNETIC FIELD

Earth is a giant magnet. Like every magnet, it is surounded by a field (zone) of magnetism. People use this field to navigate and to prove that electricity and magnetism are parts of the same force.

You can't see magnetism, but you can feel its effects. If you have ever played around with a magnet, you probably noticed that it attracts metal objects over a distance. Try to push two strong magnets together one way, and they will seem to fight against it; turn one around the opposite way, and they will pull toward each other.

The region around any magnet where its magnetism can be detected is called a magnetic field. The field gets weaker farther away from the magnet, but there are two areas in every magnet where the

The colorful Aurora lights, seen in the night sky over Earth's poles, are flowing particles in the air. Earth's magnetic field draws them over the poles.

magnetic field is especially strong. They are called the magnetic "poles." Every magnet has a north and a south pole, named according to which geographic pole of the Earth they are attracted to. Near Earth's geographic North Pole there is a magnetic pole that attracts the north pole of magnets. For this reason it is called the magnetic North Pole, or north-seeking

Magnetite

Magnetism was first discovered thousands of years ago in iron magnetite, a naturally occurring rock found all over the world. Small lumps of this rock, called lodestones (right), were used as early as 2500 B.C., when a Chinese emperor is said to have used a lodestone to guide his troops home safely through thick fog. More than 1,000 years ago lodestones were used as compasses by sailors. Magnets are named after the ancient Greek town of Magnesia, where many lodestones were found in ancient times.

pole. On the opposite side of Earth, close to the geographic South Pole, is a magnetic pole that attracts the south pole of magnets; it is called the magnetic South Pole, or south-seeking pole.

Earth's magnetic field is weak. At the surface of the planet it is hundreds of times weaker than the field produced by a small bar magnet. However, the north pole of magnetic objects will be attracted by the pull of Earth's magnetic poles and constantly point to Earth's magnetic North. Compasses made navigation possible thousands of years before satellite navigation because of this.

For a long time scientists thought Earth acted like a magnet because it had a giant magnet at its core. However, we now know that Earth has a liquid core that is too hot to hold a magnetic field (see Activity 6, pages 33–37). Scientists now believe that Earth's magnetic properties come from the link between electricity and magnetism.

In 1820 Danish physics professor Hans Christian Oersted (1777–1851) demonstrated that the needle of a compass was attracted to a wire when it had an electric current running through it. Oersted had proven that an electric current has magnetic effects. Scientists believe the motion of liquid in Earth's core may generate an electric current, which in turn creates a magnetic field.

In this activity you will use an electric current to create a small magnetic field, reproducing the historic work of Oersted.

Magnetic Earth

Earth is a giant magnet, which is why magnets always point in the same direction if allowed to swing freely. Earth's magnetic field, called the magnetosphere, extends almost 50,000 miles (110,000 kilometers) into space. Scientists do not know exactly why Earth is magnetic. They do know that Earth's North and South Poles have switched places at least twice since the planet was formed.

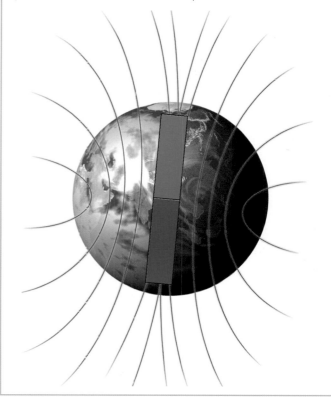

The Changing Magnetic Field

Goals

1. **Create a magnetic field.**
2. **Use a compass to find the dimensions of the magnetic field you create.**

What you will need:

- wooden board or cardboard
- straight length of rigid wire about 4 inches (10cm) long or a straightened paper clip
- two wires with alligator clips at each end
- 6-V battery
- compass
- pens of different colors

1 Bend the wire or paper clip into a V shape.

2 Tape the wire to the board with the ends of the V sticking up.

3 Clip one lead to each end of the wire.

Discovering electromagnetism

This experiment, which shows that magnetism can be produced using electricity, was first carried out in 1820 by Danish physicist Hans Christian Oersted (1777–1851). It led to the idea that magnetism and electricity are two parts of the same thing. This theory, now called electromagnetism, was further developed by English scientists Michael Faraday (1791–1867) and James Clerk Maxwell (1831–1879).

4 Clip the other end of the leads to the battery terminals.

5 Place your compass on the edge of the cardboard, and move it slowly toward the wire. As you move the compass around, use the pencil to draw arrows on the board marking the direction of the compass needle at different points.

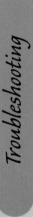

Troubleshooting

Why couldn't I find any magnetic field around the wire?

It could be that the magnetic field around the wire was not strong enough to attract the compass needle. You can increase the strength of this field by using more batteries. Make sure there are no other sources of electricity or magnetism nearby.

6 Now reverse the connections to the battery. Put the compass in the same positions as before, and with a different colored pen mark the directions it shows at each point with an arrow.

FOLLOW-UP   The changing magnetic field

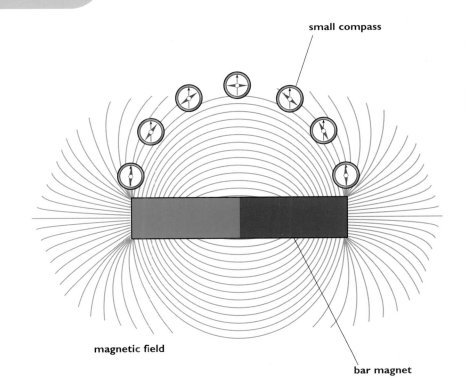

small compass

magnetic field

bar magnet

You can make this activity more precise by using a ruler to measure the distance of the different compass readings out from the wire (see photo below). It will tell you exactly how far the magnetic field extends from the wire for each battery.

If you have an ammeter, you can also use your compass to determine the strength of the magnetic field.

First, connect the battery to the wire as before. Then move the compass along the board, away from the wire until you reach a point where the

compass needle is no longer affected by the current. Measure the distance, straight across the board, from the wire to the compass. Write this number down.

Now look at the ammeter, and write down the reading it shows for the amount of current.

Now connect a second battery, and repeat the previous

steps. Write down the new distance and current.

Repeat the experiment with three and four 1.5-V batteries.

Try plotting a graph of current (on the vertical axis) against distance (on the horizontal axis). What do your results show?

If you have a bar magnet and some small compasses, you can use them to demonstrate the size of the magnetic field. Place the compasses in an arc around the magnet, as in the illustration above. Move each compass out from the magnet until it points north. Then move it back toward the magnet until the needle moves. This will be the edge of the magnetic field.

ANALYSIS
Magnetic field

When an electric current flows through a wire, it creates a magnetic field. The lines of magnetic force turn around the wire in concentric circles (circles centered on the wire itself), a bit like the ripples made when you drop a stone into a pond. The direction of the magnetic field depends on the direction of the current (right). If you imagine turning a corkscrew in the direction of the current, the lines of magnetic force turn in the direction in which your hand rotates (from north to south). If the current is flowing into the board, the magnetic field should be turning clockwise; if you reverse the current, by reversing the connections to the battery, the lines of field should be turning counterclockwise.

Oersted's experiment proved that magnetism is electricity. In fact, magnetism is produced whenever electric charges move, just as electricity is produced by the movement of magnetic fields. So, they are both part of the same force—electromagnetism.

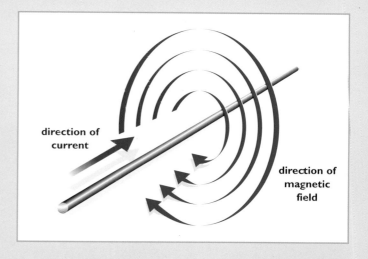

direction of current

direction of magnetic field

The magnetic field always moves in the same direction relative to the direction of the current.

The magnetic field was strongest near the wire and grew weaker the farther from the wire you moved. If you increased the current by adding more batteries, you should have found that you could now detect a magnetic field farther away from the wire.

The great turtle mystery

During mating season sea turtles travel thousands of miles to lay their eggs in the same place where they were hatched themselves. Scientists have long wondered how the tortoises find the exact speck of land they were hatched on in the vast ocean. Furthermore, the turtles always head directly for the correct island, moving across the ocean in a straight line.

Marine biologists believe that the turtles navigate with the help of Earth's magnetic field. In the same way

many other animals (including bees, pigeons, whales, and dolphins) are also believed to use Earth's magnetic field to navigate.

Scientists have found tiny pieces of iron magnetite inside the brains of these animals and believe the crystals act like tiny compass needles, helping the animals follow Earth's magnetic field. Some scientists believe humans may also be able to detect Earth's magnetism. Many people can correctly point to north (or south) after being blindfolded and spun around.

ACTIVITY 9
ELECTROMAGNETISM

Speakers, televisions, computers, and motors use electromagnets. Unlike refrigerator bar magnets, electromagnets use electricity to generate a magnetic field, and they can be turned on and off.

As scientists began to experiment more with electricity and magnetism, they realized that there could be a possible link between the two. The first to discover such a connection was Danish physicist Hans Christian Oersted (see Activity 7, pages 43 to 49).

In 1820 Oersted discovered accidentally that a wire with an electric current running through it could deflect a compass from the Earth's North Pole. He realized that the electricity flowing in the wire generated its own magnetic field, and it was disrupting the nearby compass.

This particle accelerator is used to study the particles that make up atoms. The accelerator uses very strong electric and magnetic fields to trap the particles and move them around so they can be properly studied.

Shortly after this French physicist and mathematician André-Marie Ampère (1775–1836) worked out in detail exactly how an electric current produces a magnetic field and summarized his results in an equation now called Ampère's rule. Although devised 150 years ago, this law is still used by scientists and engineers.

The two forces of electricity and magnetism were linked into the single force of electromagnetism by British physicist James Clerk Maxwell (1831–1879). Maxwell's four equations explain how electric currents produce magnetic fields. The equations state that: electric charges produce electric fields; magnetic poles always occur in pairs (north and south); changing, or moving, magnetic fields produce electric currents; and changes in electric currents produce changes in magnetic fields.

ELECTROMAGNETISM IN ACTION

These early experiments have led to some very important practical uses. Electromagnets are now used in many electronic devices, including loudspeakers, tape players, computers, and one of the 20th century's most entertaining inventions: television.

In some of the experiments in this book you may have used an ammeter to measure current. This instrument also uses electromagnets. Traditional meters (with pointers that move across a scale) are sometimes called moving-coil meters. If you look at the base of the pointer, where it pivots around, you can see why they have this name. The pointer is attached to a coil of copper wire placed between the poles of a permanent magnet. When an electric current flows through the coil, it becomes an electromagnet. The magnetic field produced by the electromagnet pulls on the field of the permanent magnet and makes the coil rotate. The greater the current, the bigger the force on the coil, the more it rotates, and the more the pointer moves.

In this activity you can experiment with using an electric field to produce a magnetic field by building your own electromagnet.

Electromagnetic TV

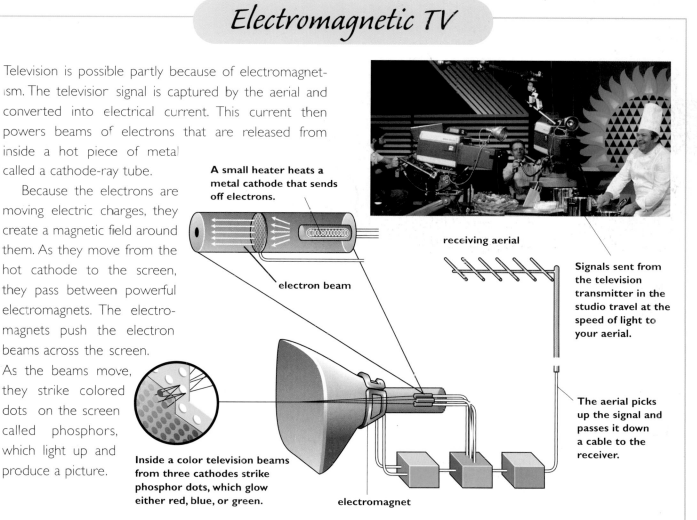

Television is possible partly because of electromagnetism. The television signal is captured by the aerial and converted into electrical current. This current then powers beams of electrons that are released from inside a hot piece of metal called a cathode-ray tube.

Because the electrons are moving electric charges, they create a magnetic field around them. As they move from the hot cathode to the screen, they pass between powerful electromagnets. The electromagnets push the electron beams across the screen. As the beams move, they strike colored dots on the screen called phosphors, which light up and produce a picture.

A small heater heats a metal cathode that sends off electrons.

electron beam

Inside a color television beams from three cathodes strike phosphor dots, which glow either red, blue, or green.

receiving aerial

Signals sent from the television transmitter in the studio travel at the speed of light to your aerial.

The aerial picks up the signal and passes it down a cable to the receiver.

electromagnet

Build an Electromagnet

Goals

1. **Build an electromagnet and test its strength.**
2. **Demonstrate the principles of electromagnetism.**

What you will need:

- *iron nail*
- *copper wire*
- *a 6-V battery*
- *electrical connector leads with alligator clips*
- *10–30 paper clips*

1 Demonstrate that a nail is not magnetic by holding it to a pile of paper clips. You will not be able to pick up any of the paper clips with the nail.

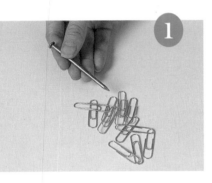

2 Take a 1-foot (30-cm) length of copper wire, and coil it about 20 times around an iron nail, leaving about 2 inches (5cm) of wire sticking out at either end.

3 Take the leads and attach one alligator clip from each lead to each of the wire ends sticking out from the nail. Connect the two free alligator clips to the terminals of a 6-V battery.

Electromagnetic gauges

Car fuel gauges use electromagnets to let the driver know how much gasoline is left in the tank. In the fuel gauge an electromagnet sits inside a permanent magnet. A current flows through the electromagnet, which then turns toward the permanent magnet, moving a pointer. The amount it turns depends on the strength of the current. Inside the gas tank a float moves up and down with the level of gas and controls the current flowing through the meter. When the fuel level is high, a high current flows, creating a powerful electro-magnet that pulls the pointer all the way over to read FULL.

Troubleshooting

What if the nail electromagnet only picks up a few paper clips?

The most common reason for the electromagnet to be weak is that the coils are not wound very tightly, or that there are not enough coils. Start over with another nail, wrap the coils tighter, and make sure there are at least 30 or 40 coils around the nail.

4 Now hold your electromagnet close to the pile of paper clips. You should find that the nail has become magnetic and will now pick up the paper clips.

5 See how many paper clips you can pick up.

FOLLOW-UP   Build an electromagnet

Make a more powerful electromagnet by increasing the number of coils in the wire, then experiment with determining the magnetic power of a different number of coils. Start with a single coil wrapped around the nail, then try 10 coils, then 100 coils. Each time you increase the number of coils, compare the strength of the electromagnetic field by testing how many paper clips the magnet can pick up.

As the number of wire coils around the nail increases, you should be able to pick up more paper clips because the electromagnet will now be more powerful.

Change the voltage
Experiment to find out if voltage makes any difference in the strength of the electromagnet. Connect your electromagnet to two 1.5-V batteries connected in series to get a total of 3 volts. Does the strength of the electromagnet change? Use only flashlight batteries, and do not use more than 6 volts. Larger batteries create too much current and can be very dangerous.

Iron vs. aluminum
Experiment to find out if the type of material used for the core makes a difference in the strength of the magnetic field. For example, roll some aluminum foil into a tight tube, and coil the wire around it instead of the nail. What happens? You could also try using a plastic core, made from a pen, or a wooden core, made from a pencil.

Build a solenoid
A solenoid is another type of electromagnet. Solenoids are used in many types of electronic equipment to move small pieces of metal.

To build a solenoid, you will need: a drinking straw, wire, battery, connectors, and a small nail (or a straightened paper clip) that will slide inside the straw easily.

Wrap 100 turns of wire around the straw, leaving about 3 inches (7.5cm) of straight wire at each end. Place the nail or paper clip at one end of the straw, and touch the straight wire to the terminals of the battery. The nail should move.

Try replacing the nail with a thin permanent magnet. You can move this magnet in and out by changing the direction of the magnetic field in the solenoid. (Be careful if you try putting a magnet in your solenoid, since the magnet can shoot out.)

Magnetic field
You can look at an electromagnet's magnetic field with iron filings. Buy some iron filings, or find your own iron filings by running a magnet through playground or beach sand. Put a light dusting of filings on a sheet of paper, and place the paper over a magnet. Tap the paper lightly, and the filings will align with the magnetic field.

ANALYSIS

Electromagnetism

When you connect a battery to a wire in a circuit, you are creating both an electric circuit and a magnetic field. This magnetic field is caused by the flow of electrons through the wire and will occur no matter what material the wire is wrapped around.

As you saw in Activity 8 (pages 44 to 49), a circular magnetic field develops around the wire. The field is perpendicular to the wire and weakens as it moves out from the wire. The direction of the field is the same as the flow of current and changes as the current changes.

Because the magnetic field that develops around the wire is circular and perpendicular to the wire, you can easily make the field stronger by coiling the wire. The more coils you make, the stronger the magnetic field.

As you may remember from Activity 6 (pages 33 to 37), in magnetic materials like iron and steel the electrons inside the atoms join

Loudspeakers and megaphones use electromagnets to pull a cone inside the speaker inward or outward, depending on the direction of current moving through a wire wrapped around the cone. The vibrations of the cone send sound signals through the air.

André-Marie Ampère

In the 1820s French physicist and mathematician André-Marie Ampère (1775–1836) became the first person to figure out a precise formula for the amount of magnetism produced when an electric current flows through a wire. This discovery laid the foundations of modern electromagnetism. Ampère also built the first instrument for measuring electric current: the galvanometer. His work was an important contribution to the history of physics. The unit of electrical current, the amp (A), is named in his honor.

together to form areas that can become magnetized, called magnetic domains. When a wire is wrapped around the metal and a current is run through it, a magnetic field is generated. That causes the domains to line up facing the same direction, and the metal becomes a temporary magnet. When the current is switched off, the magnetic field disappears, the domains scramble up again, and the iron is no longer magnetic.

Most magnets are either permanent or temporary magnets, but in electromagnets the magnetism can be "turned on" and "turned off" by controlling the flow of current. It is this ability to turn the magnet on and off that has made electromagnets so useful in electronic devices.

ACTIVITY 10
EDDY CURRENTS

When a conductor, like aluminum, moves past a magnet, an electromagnetic current is created in the conductor. This is called an eddy current, and it is used in some surprising, everyday devices.

In Activity 9: Electromagnetism and Activity 8: Magnetic Field you experimented with using electricity to generate a magnetic field. However, because electricity and magnetism are really two types of the same force, you can also use magnetism to generate electricity. The process of using magnetism to generate electricity is called electromagnetic induction, and it can be very useful.

ELECTROMAGNETIC INDUCTION

When a conductor, such as a wire or a piece of metal, swings between the two poles of a magnet, the changing magnetic field created by the movement

Automobile speedometers use an electromagnetic induction force called an eddy current to turn a disk and move the speedometer needle.

of the conductor between the north and south poles of the magnet pushes the electrons in the conductor around in circular currents. If you could see these currents, their movement would look like the ripples, or eddies, in a pond, so they are called eddy currents. Eddy currents form an electromagnetic field that flows through the wire.

One of the the first people to experiment with eddy currents was Estonian physicist Heinrich Lenz (1804–1865). Lenz found that if you move a magnet

Maglev train

Unlike conventional trains, which rest on the track as they move and are slowed by friction, magnetic levitation (maglev) trains hover above the track, suspended by a magnetic field. Powerful electromagnets create this magnetic field.

Maglev trains use a linear induction motor, which consists of an electromagnet in the locomotive that propels the train past flat coils of copper or aluminum, called reaction rails, that are placed inside existing railroad track.

The idea of using maglev for transportation was first proposed in 1914, but it remains experimental. Japanese engineers built a prototype called the ML-500 in 1979 that achieved a speed of 321 miles per hour (513km/h). There are plans to build full-scale maglev railroads in several countries, including Japan and Germany.

electromagnets

near a conductor (or move a conductor through a magnetic field), the eddy current generated in the conductor will move in the opposite direction from the magnetic field. The opposing currents will slow the movement of the conductor.

In general, the larger the magnetic field, and the larger the conductor, the greater the eddy currents will be, and the more the conductor will be slowed.

USES FOR EDDY CURRENTS

Electromagnetic induction is used in a type of electric motor called an induction motor. In an induction motor a piece of metal swings between electromagnets, producing a magnetic field. The magnetic field then creates eddy currents in the piece of metal, and they make it rotate. The rotating metal is used to power a piece of machinery.

Another type of induction motor uses electromagnets in a straight line. When the electric current is switched on, the electromagnets produce eddy currents in a piece of metal, and the metal shoots straight past the magnets. This is called a linear (which means straight line) induction motor, and it is best known as the power source used in maglev trains (see box above).

Eddy currents are also used to dampen unwanted movements. If your school has a mechanical balance, ask a teacher if you can look inside the mechanism. You may be able to see a thin metal strip moving between two magnets. It creates an eddy current that will slow down unwanted movement from the scales.

Automobile speedometers are another common use of eddy currents. A rotating magnet connected to the car's drive system spins next to an aluminum disk. As the magnet turns, it causes eddy currents in the aluminum disk. They produce a magnetic force that makes the disk (and the speedometer needle) rotate. The faster the car goes, the more the magnet spins, the stronger the eddy currents, and the more the speedometer needle rotates.

Eddy currents also have some unwanted effects. They are generated as a side effect in transformers and other electrical machines that use electromagnets. The eddy currents pull against the electromagnetic field and cause a loss of power. To combat this, thin strips of metal are used to build the transformer instead of one solid piece of metal. The strips are separated by insulating glue, which holds the eddy currents around the strips. This reduces the currents, thereby reducing the power loss.

Slowing with Eddy Currents

ACTIVITY

Goals

1. **Create eddy currents.**
2. **Compare the strength of the eddy currents created in different materials.**
3. **Use eddy currents to slow movement.**

What you will need:

- *tripod*
- *wooden dowel*
- *string and modeling clay*
- *large bar magnet*
- *stopwatch or clock with a second hand*
- *several disks of different materials (metals and insulators of different kinds); they should be approximately the same size.*

1. Ask an adult to drill a hole in one end of the dowel.

2. Hang the dowel from the tripod so that it swings freely back and forth in a straight line, like a pendulum. There should be about an inch between the end of the dowel and the table top.

Eddy heating

Induction heating is a method for providing fast, consistent heat used for manufacturing metals or other conductive materials. In induction heating current is sent through a coil, generating a magnetic field.

A piece of metal is placed in the center of the coil. The magnetic field causes eddy currents in the metal that generate heat. By varying the amount of current, parts of the metal can be heated to exact temperatures without any contact with the coil.

3. Place the magnet under the dowel so that the dowel hangs over the middle of the magnet.

4 Use modeling clay or tape to attach one of the disks to the bottom of the dowel.

5 Place a ruler next to the stand, and align the 0 mark on the ruler with the end of the magnet. Pull the disk back to the 10-inch (25cm) mark and release it. At the same moment start the stop watch.

7 Repeat the experiment with disks made from the other materials. Try to use a wide selection of different types of metal and other materials. Time how long it takes each disk to stop.

6 Time how long it takes the disk to come to a complete rest.

Troubleshooting

What if I can't notice a change in the time it takes different materials to slow down?

You might have to use a stronger magnet—horseshoe magnets work well. Also, make sure you are using a variety of both metals and nonmetals.

FOLLOW-UP

Slowing with eddy currents

You can increase the strength of the magnetic field by using two bar magnets. Place them about 1 inch (2.5cm) apart, with the north pole of one facing the south pole of the other across the gap. Be careful to position your pendulum so that it swings in the gap between the two magnets.

Now repeat the activity. What changes do you notice in the swing?

Slowing a magnet in a pipe

There is another simple experiment that you can perform that will demonstrate how eddy currents pull against a magnetic field.

For this demonstration you will need: 2-foot (60cm) long plastic pipe, 2-foot (60cm) long aluminum pipe, two identical permanent magnets (small pellet-shaped magnets work well), a wall or board, and tape.

Tape both pipes next to each other against a wall or board. The pipes should be a few inches apart and about 6 inches (15cm) above the ground. Both pipes should be at

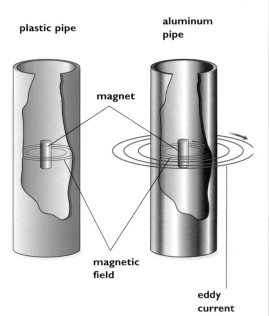

exactly the same height. Now hold one magnet over each pipe, and let them both drop at exactly the same time. Which magnet hits the ground first?

Repeat the experiment with tubes made from different materials, such as copper and cardboard. Which materials do the magnets pass through

ANALYSIS

Eddy currents

A permanent magnet creates a magnetic field all around it. When you move a conductor, like a piece of metal or a wire, past the magnet, a magnetic field is created in the conductor.

In your activity eddy currents formed in the disks as they swung between the poles of the magnet. These currents flow in the opposite direction from the current in the magnet, and the

interaction of the two magnetic fields slows the disks and pulls them to a stop. The better the conductor, the stronger the eddy current, and the faster the disk will come to a stop.

You should have found that disks made from good conductors, such as copper and aluminum, slowed down fastest, followed by poor conductors, like steel and nickel. Eddy currents do not form in insulators, such as plastic and cardboard, so disks made from these materials would not be slowed down and should have taken the longest times to come to a stop.

According to Lenz's law, eddy currents move in the opposite direction from whatever created them. Because they were created by the movement of the magnet, the eddy currents in the disks move opposite the magnetic field of the magnet. In short, the disks "run after" the magnet in an attempt to catch up with it because that would eliminate the cause of the eddy currents.

Slowing the pendulum

As you can see in this illustration of the activity, the swing of the pendulum is slowed by the interaction between the eddy currents in the conductor and the magnetic field of the magnet. The eddy currents are attracted to the magnetic field, and this helps slow the swing of the pendulum. Materials that are good conductors will form more eddy currents and will thus slow down faster.

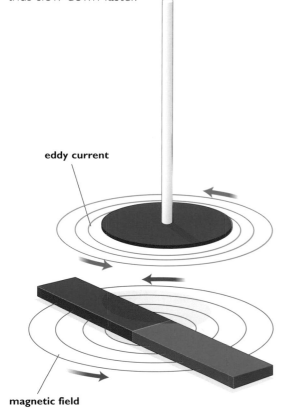

eddy current

magnetic field

This trainee engineer (above) is examining the inside of the induction coil of a large generator at a Florida school for nuclear submarine sailors.

If you performed the follow-up activity with the two tubes and two magnets, you would have found that the magnet fell more slowly in the metal tube than in the plastic tube. As the magnet passed through a given section of the metal tube, the changing magnetic field caused by the magnet's fall made eddy currents form in that section of the tube. The eddy currents that were formed then exerted a force on the falling magnet. The direction of this force (up) was opposite that of the magnet's fall (down). This upward pull, or magnetic repulsion, slowed the magnet's fall. Because a plastic tube is not a good conductor, the magnet in that tube was not slowed as much.

If you tried the follow-up with a variety of tubes made from different materials, you should have found that the best conductors, like copper and aluminum, were the most effective in slowing the magnet's fall.

GLOSSARY

atom: Unit of an element. In an element all the atoms share the same number of subatomic particles called protons and electrons.

ammeter: A device used to measure current in units called amps.

amp: Properly called an ampere, an amp is the unit used to measure current.

anatomist: A scientist who studies the shapes of the different parts of living things, how they fit together, and what they are for.

cathode-ray tube: An empty (vacuum) tube that sends out a stream of electrons. In television sets the electrons are projected onto the screen to light up certain points and form a picture. The electron stream is controlled by a magnetic field inside the tube.

chemical energy: A form of energy that is released by a chemical reaction in which bonds between atoms break and re-form.

circuit: The path that electricity travels. Electricity can only flow around a complete circuit.

circuit board: A plastic board on which an electric circuit is laid out. The circuit is etched onto the board, and the electric components are screwed onto it.

circuit breaker: A switch that flips off automatically when there is a problem (such as too much current flowing) in a circuit. It protects the appliances within the circuit.

components: The parts of a circuit, such as batteries, lights, buzzers, and so on.

concentric circles: Different-sized circles with the same center point.

conductor: A substance that allows electricity to travel through it easily.

Curie point: The temperature at which normally permanently magnetic metals lose their magnetism.

current: The amount of a flow of electrical energy, or charge, in a substance. Measured in amps.

domain: Tiny areas in a metal that behave like magnets, and that all have to be lined up in the same way

for the whole piece of metal to be magnetic.

electric charge: A particular amount of electricity in a substance—either extra electrons or fewer electrons.

electrode: A conductor used to make contact with a nonmetallic part of a circuit.

electrolyte: A nonmetal electric conductor, often a liquid or paste.

electromagnet: A core of magnetic material, such as iron, surrounded by a coil of wire. When an electric current is passed through the wire, the core becomes magnetic.

electromotive force (emf): Another word for voltage—the force that sets electricity in motion.

electron: A particle that makes up part of an atom. Electricity is the flow of electrons.

electrical energy: The energy provided by the flow of electrons.

ferromagnet: Materials that are noticeably more magnetic than most others.

Ferromagnetic elements include cobalt, nickel, and iron. Ferromagnetic compounds include magnetite (an iron oxide) and chromite (a compound made up of iron, chromium, and oxygen).

flammable: Something that catches fire easily.

fuse: A wire, or thin metal, in an electric circuit that melts when too much electricity is flowing through it. It acts as a safety device to protect the other components in the circuit.

galvanometer: An instrument that measures small amounts of electric current using a magnetic needle or a coil in a magnetic field.

generator: A machine that changes mechanical energy into electrical energy.

geologist: A scientist who studies the history of Earth through its rocks.

induction: The process in which a conductor becomes electrified, a substance becomes magnetized, or an electromotive force is produced in a circuit by changing the magnetic field.

insulator: A substance that does not conduct electricity very well. Insulators are used to protect conductors.

iron filing: Tiny pieces, or shavings, of iron.

landmass: An area of land—usually a very large area, such as a continent.

magnetic field: The area around a magnet where magnetism can be detected.

magnetite: A naturally occuring magnetic rock, also called lodestone.

motor: A machine that changes electrical or chemical energy into mechanical energy.

permanent magnet: A material that does not lose its magnetism naturally.

pole: One of the two ends of a magnet, the north and south poles.

power: A source of energy.

power plant: A building in which a generator produces electricity for use by homes, offices, and industries.

potential difference: The difference in the amount of electrons at two ends of a circuit. Electrons will flow around a circuit from the end with more electrons to the end with fewer electrons.

That is the potential difference.

resistance: The extent to which a substance prevents electricity traveling through it. Substances with high resistance are good insulators, and substances with low resistance are good conductors.

solenoid: A coil of wire that acts like a magnet when a current is passed through it. A movable piece of metal is drawn into the coil when a current flows, and it is used as a switch.

static electricity: An electric charge that does not move from one place to another.

temporary magnet: A substance that is not naturally magnetic but can be made magnetic by placing it near or rubbing it with a permanent magnet.

terminal: In batteries the places where electricity flows to and from.

transformer: An electrical device used to change current into voltage.

voltage: A measurement of potential difference.

voltmeter: A device used to measure voltage in units called volts.

SET INDEX